The Cannabis Debate

ISSUES

Volume 80

Editor

Craig Donnellan

Independence

Educational Publishers
Cambridge

First published by Independence
PO Box 295
Cambridge CB1 3XP
England

British Library Cataloguing in Publication Data
The Cannabis Debate – (Issues Series)
I. Donnellan, Craig II. Series
362.2'95

ISBN 1 86168 275 1

Printed in Great Britain
MWL Print Group Ltd

Typeset by
Claire Boyd

Cover
The illustration on the front cover is by
Pumpkin House.

CONTENTS

Chapter One: The Facts of Cannabis

Cannabis/Dope/Marijuana/Skunk/Grass	1
One in three young men use cannabis	2
Drug misuse	2
Cannabis trends	3
Drug use among young adults	3
Cannabis	4
Cannabis – facts and urban myths	6
So how many people use cannabis in the UK?	6
Cannabis economy brings in £11bn	8
Cannabis misconceptions	9
Drugs and harm	10
The cannabis market	11
Cannabis – the lies and the truth	12
Cannabis – a soft drug?	13
Cannabis and mental health	14
Cannabis-related harms on health	15
Addiction	15
Cannabis deaths	16
Drug-related poisoning deaths	16
Cannabis link to psychosis	17
Cannabis for the GP	18
Cannabis is blamed as cause of man's death	20

Drug-driving	21
Medical use of cannabis approved	22

Chapter Two: The Legal Debate

The legal position on cannabis	23
Cannabis reclassification	24
Cannabis and the law	27
Simple and powerful rebuttals of common arguments	28
Government ads aim to end confusion	29
ACPO publish cannabis enforcement guidelines	30
Policing cannabis	31
Seizures of selected drugs	31
Home cultivation of cannabis	32
Mixed signals	33
Life after reclassification	34
Use of cannabis for alleviation of MS symptoms	35
Medical cannabis	36
Cannabis-based medicines	38
Key Facts	40
Additional Resources	41
Index	42
Acknowledgements	44

Introduction

The Cannabis Debate is the eightieth volume in the **Issues** series. The aim of this series is to offer up-to-date information about important issues in our world.

The Cannabis Debate examines the prevalence and use of cannabis and the debate on health, medicinal and legal issues.

The information comes from a wide variety of sources and includes:
Government reports and statistics
Newspaper reports and features
Magazine articles and surveys
Web site material
Literature from lobby groups
and charitable organisations.

It is hoped that, as you read about the many aspects of the issues explored in this book, you will critically evaluate the information presented. It is important that you decide whether you are being presented with facts or opinions. Does the writer give a biased or an unbiased report? If an opinion is being expressed, do you agree with the writer?

The Cannabis Debate offers a useful starting-point for those who need convenient access to information about the many issues involved. However, it is only a starting-point. At the back of the book is a list of organisations which you may want to contact for further information.

*****

Cannabis/Dope/ Marijuana/Skunk/Grass

Information from RELEASE

What is it?

Cannabis is one of the world's most commonly used leisure drugs. It's estimated that at least one person in 20 in the UK has used it.

Cannabis comes from the plant *Cannabis Sativa*, a relative of the hop plant which is used for making beer. Its leaves are made up of 4-8 smaller lance-shaped leaves with saw-toothed edges. When smoked, it has a sweet, herbal smell.

Cannabis comes in three main forms: cannabis resin, marijuana/ grass and cannabis oil.

What does it look like?

Cannabis resin is a dark to light brown substance which is scraped off the surface of the plant and pressed into a solid lump. Resin is often bought in street quantities from a sixteenth to a quarter of an ounce, but regular users may buy greater quantities. It comes from the upper leaves and the small leaves on the stem of the plant. Resin is sometimes taken on its own, but more often it is mixed with tobacco and smoked.

Marijuana or grass is the dried leaves and/or flowering tops of the cannabis plant. It looks like dried herbs and is often mixed with stems and seeds. It is also often mixed with tobacco and smoked.

> *Smoking is by far the most common method of taking cannabis. However, it can also be eaten, either on its own, or in a variety of ways ranging from tea to cakes*

Cannabis oil is a treacly liquid, refined from the resin or (less frequently) from the plant itself. Oil is often thought to be the strongest form of cannabis. It's smoked with ordinary tobacco, either by mixing it with the tobacco or by smearing it on cigarette paper which is then used to roll up tobacco.

How is it used?

Smoking is by far the most common method of taking cannabis. However, it can also be eaten, either on its own, or in a variety of ways ranging from tea to cakes. The effects of eating cannabis can be less pre-dictable because people often don't measure the quantity carefully, or may not know how much of the drug is in the food.

What are the effects?

The mind-altering ingredient is a substance called *delta 9 tetra-hydrocannabinol* (THC). The main types of cannabis vary greatly in their strength, depending on the concentration of THC. There's usually a higher concentration in the resin than in the leaves of the plant.

The effects of the drug also depend upon your mood, your surroundings and the amount taken. The drug may bring on feelings of contentment, relaxation and happiness. You may feel giggly. Many people don't experience much when they first use the drug, and have to learn what effects to look out for.

Is it addictive?

Cannabis is not physically addictive. A minority of users can come to depend on the drug's effects – i.e. become psychologically dependent.

Are there any side effects?

Cannabis can cause tiredness, reddening of the eyes, dry mouth, an increase in your pulse rate and a drop in blood pressure. While the drug effect lasts, it is harder to concentrate. For example, driving may be difficult and dangerous.

Some people, particularly those taking high doses, may feel quite edgy. They may even experience short-term panic. After a short time, most unpleasant effects should subside.

What are the risks?

Smoking the drug has all the problems associated with smoking tobacco, such as bronchitis, lung cancer and heart disease. The effects of cannabis may cause special risks for people with breathing or mental health problems.

Drug testing

Cannabis can be detected in urine samples (the usual method of testing) for a good while after use. Occasional use can be detected on average for up to 7 days after last use. Heavy cannabis use can be detected for up to 12 weeks in some cases it may even be longer. The detection periods vary depending on the testing equipment used, your weight and amount of cannabis taken.

■ The above information is from a factsheet produced by RELEASE. Visit their web site for further details at www.release.org.uk

© RELEASE

One in three young men use cannabis

In 2001/02, 15 per cent of men and 9 per cent of women aged 16 to 59 in England and Wales said that they had taken an illicit drug in the previous year. Among young people (those aged 16 to 24), 35 per cent of men and 24 per cent of women said they had done so in the previous year.

The most commonly used drug by young people was cannabis, which had been used by 33 per cent of young men and 21 per cent of young women in the previous year.

Ecstasy was the most commonly used Class A drug, with higher use among the 16- to 24-year-olds than those aged 25 to 59. In 2001/02, 9 per cent of men and 4 per cent of women aged 16 to 24 had used ecstasy in the previous year.

Since 1996 there has been an increase in the use of cocaine among young people, especially among young men. In contrast the use of amphetamines and LSD has declined.

Drug offences accounted for 2 per cent of recorded crime in England and Wales in 2002/03. Drug offences can cover a range of activities, including unlawful production, supply, and most commonly, possession of illegal substances.

In 2001, the total number of drug seizures in the United Kingdom rose by 5 per cent to 131,000, following two years of decline. Seizures were 21,000 lower than in the last peak in 1998. HM Customs and the National Crime Squad generally seized larger amounts while local police forces made a greater number of smaller seizures.

Cannabis accounted for 71 per cent of the total number of seizures in 2001. In terms of the quantity of drugs seized, while the amount of cocaine seized fell by 28 per cent in 2001 to just under 3 tonnes, the amounts of the other main Class A drugs recovered all rose.

© Crown copyright

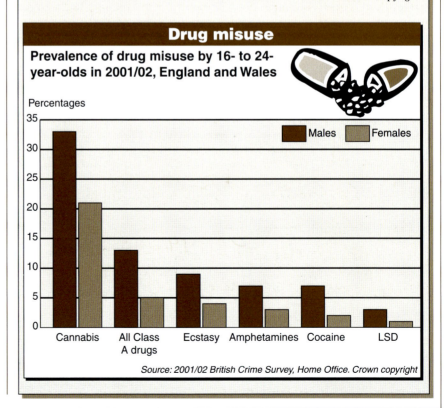

Drug misuse

Prevalence of drug misuse by 16- to 24-year-olds in 2001/02, England and Wales

Percentages

■ Males ■ Females

Cannabis | All Class A drugs | Ecstasy | Amphetamines | Cocaine | LSD

Source: 2001/02 British Crime Survey, Home Office. Crown copyright

Cannabis trends

Trends in the drug situation

Cannabis remains the most commonly used drug in the EU, with many countries reporting lifetime prevalence rates in excess of 20% of the general population. A conservative estimate would suggest that at least one in every five adults in the EU has tried the drug.

Indicators suggest that cannabis use has been increasing across the EU, although this increase appears to have stabilised in some countries, albeit at what can generally be considered to be historically high levels. Some evidence of a convergence in patterns of use is also found, although rates still vary considerably, with France, Spain and the United Kingdom, in particular, reporting relatively high levels of use, and Finland, Sweden and Portugal reporting comparatively low figures. In all countries, estimates of the prevalence of recent use (last-year prevalence) among the adult population remain below 10%. When young adults are considered, rates of use rise considerably. In all countries, recent use (last-year) prevalence peaks in the 15- to 25-year age group, with France, Germany, Ireland, Spain and the United Kingdom all reporting that over 20% of this age group have used cannabis in the last 12 months. Lifetime use estimates are higher, with most countries reporting lifetime prevalence estimates of between 20% and 35% among young people. The number of people using cannabis on a regular basis is small in overall population terms (generally less than 1%), although higher rates of regular use may be found among young people, and in particular among young men.

> *Indicators suggest that cannabis use has been increasing across the EU at what can generally be considered to be historically high levels*

A worrying trend is the increasing frequency with which cannabis is mentioned in the context of the treatment demand indicator (TDI). In many countries, cannabis is now the drug most frequently reported after heroin, and a steady increase in cannabis-related demand for treatment can be observed. Caution is needed in interpreting these data as a number of factors are likely to be important here. This issue is currently being explored by an EMCDDA technical working group and will be the focus of a publication in 2004.

In most EU countries, the majority of reports for drug law offences are related to cannabis. Cannabis seizures have exhibited an increasing trend over the last decade, although there are signs that seizures have stabilised. Europe remains the world's biggest market for cannabis resin, with as much as three-quarters of the world total of cannabis resin being seized within the borders of the EU. Many countries also now report that herbal cannabis is being grown within the EU. The content of THC (tetrahydrocannabinol), the main active chemical in cannabis, varies greatly in street-level samples. On average, the THC content of resin and herbal cannabis is similar (5-14% and 5-11% respectively), although some samples of both forms of the drug are found to have a very high THC content.

■ The above information is from *The State of the Drugs Problem in the European Union and Norway*, Annual Report 2003 of the European Monitoring Centre for Drugs and Drug Addiction (EMCDDA).

© EMCDDA

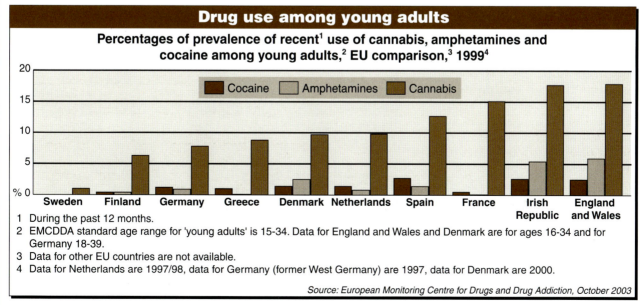

Drug use among young adults

Percentages of prevalence of recent[1] use of cannabis, amphetamines and cocaine among young adults,[2] EU comparison,[3] 1999[4]

Legend: Cocaine, Amphetamines, Cannabis

Countries (left to right): Sweden, Finland, Germany, Greece, Denmark, Netherlands, Spain, France, Irish Republic, England and Wales

1 During the past 12 months.
2 EMCDDA standard age range for 'young adults' is 15-34. Data for England and Wales and Denmark are for ages 16-34 and for Germany 18-39.
3 Data for other EU countries are not available.
4 Data for Netherlands are 1997/98, data for Germany (former West Germany) are 1997, data for Denmark are 2000.

Source: European Monitoring Centre for Drugs and Drug Addiction, October 2003

Cannabis

Information from DrugScope

Bhang, black, blast, blow, blunts, Bob Hope, bush, dope, draw, ganga, grass, hash, hashish, hemp, herb, marijuana, pot, puff, Northern Lights, resin, sensi, sensemilla, skunk, smoke, spliff, wacky backy, weed, zero etc.

Some names are based on country of origin such as Afghan, Colombian, homegrown, Lebanese, Moroccan, Pakistani etc. Cannabis comes from *Cannabis sativa*, a bushy plant that grows in many parts of the world and is also cultivated in the UK. The main active ingredients in cannabis are the tetrahydro-cannabinols (THC). These are the chemicals that cause the effect on the brain.

Different forms of cannabis come from different parts of the plant and have different strengths. 'Hashish' or 'hash' is the commonest form found in the UK. It is resin scraped or rubbed from the dried plant and then pressed into brown/black blocks. It is mostly imported from Morocco, Pakistan, the Lebanon, Afghanistan or Nepal. Herbal cannabis is made from the chopped, dried leaves of the plant. It is also known as 'grass', 'bush' and 'ganga' and in America as 'marijuana' and is imported from Africa, South America, Thailand and the West Indies. Some is 'homegrown' and cultivated in this country, sometimes on a large scale to sell but usually by individuals in their homes or greenhouses for their own use.

Herbal cannabis is usually not as strong as the resin form. However, some particularly strong herbal forms such as 'sinsemilla' and 'skunk' have recently been cultivated in Holland and this country.

Cannabis oil is the least common form of cannabis found in the UK. It is made by percolating a solvent through the resin.

In the UK cannabis is usually smoked rolled into a cigarette or joint, often with tobacco. The herbal form is sometimes made into a cigarette without using tobacco. Cannabis is also sometimes smoked in a pipe, brewed into a tea or cooked into cakes.

Hemp is the fibre of the cannabis plant. For centuries to the present day it has been used to make all sorts of products including rope, mats, clothing, cooking oil, fuel, fishing nets, cosmetics, herbal remedies, paints and varnishes.

Prevalence goes up

Cannabis is the most widely used illegal drug in the UK and easily the illegal drug most likely to have been tried by young people. Recent surveys, such as the *British Crime Survey* (2002), show that though overall use may be falling among teenagers, cannabis has been used by over half (55 per cent) of young men and over a third (44 per cent) of young women aged 16 to 29 years. Twenty-seven per cent of this age range have used in the last year and 14 per cent in the last month. In total over 8.5 million people have tried it at least once and roughly 2 million use it on an occasional basis.

Perhaps because of its wide-spread use and lack of obvious ill-effects, there has been much debate about the legal status of cannabis. In general, government-commissioned reports in the English-speaking world have recommended relaxation of the existing cannabis laws. These views are shared by a number of academics, politicians and senior law enforcers.

During the 1990s, on the back of renewed interest about drug use among young people, the cannabis reform lobby took various guises ranging from the Green Party and the UK Cannabis Alliance to supportive editorials in the broadsheets and in particular the pro-reform campaign of the *Independent on Sunday*. The Liberal Democrats have supported legal changes and lobbied for a Royal Commission to explore the issues and more conservative newspapers such as the *Times* and *Daily Telegraph* have called for liberalisation of the cannabis laws.

The public and political debate

The trend in UK public opinion, particularly among under-35s, is towards support for decriminalisation of cannabis use (but not for other illegal drugs) though not necessarily full-scale legalisation. There is also widespread support among all age groups for doctors being able to prescribe cannabis to patients. Many commentators see politicians as lagging far behind public opinion.

The key issues

The debate about the law on cannabis centres on a number of important legal and social issues concerning civil liberties and personal choice, legal coherence and international agreements. In addition, there are arguments about the link between cannabis and use of other drugs, whether law changes would increase or decrease drug problems and exactly what changes might take place.

Perhaps the most hotly debated social issue is that of civil liberties and personal choice. This argument hinges on the point at which it is appropriate to legislate to stop individuals from doing something that may do them harm and/or may result in substantial costs to society, even though such legislation is an infringement of personal choice. An example of a relatively recent decision of this sort is seen in the laws that make seat-belt wearing compulsory. The argument in favour was that the damage to individuals and the human and economic cost to society were too great, the loss of personal liberty relatively small and that the former outweighed the latter. In the case of alcohol and tobacco the balance is seen to fall the other way – on the side of individual choice rather than costs to individuals and society. The question is where the balance should fall in relation to cannabis and whether a criminal prosecution is warranted in face of the known risks.

Underlying this issue is fierce debate about exactly how dangerous cannabis use actually is. While some people see cannabis as a relatively harmless drug others see it as having detrimental impact on individual users and wider society.

The impact of criminalising otherwise law-abiding mainly young citizens, the detrimental impact on their future lives and careers (for example losing jobs or not being able to work in jobs with children) and damage to the relationship between police and communities also need to be taken into account. Concerns over such issues were highlighted sharply by serious rioting in London, Bristol and Liverpool in the early 1980s, when the police were accused of misusing their power to investigate drug offences to harass black youngsters on the streets.

Different forms of cannabis come from different parts of the plant and have different strengths. 'Hashish' or 'hash' is the commonest form found in the UK

A second area of debate is not about drugs per se, but about the law. Some judges and serving senior policemen have themselves expressed concern about the viability of catching and prosecuting cannabis users, highlighting the rapid growth of cautioning for simple possession of cannabis which represents by far the majority of drug offences. In Lambeth, London, for example, police, with the tacit backing of the Metropolitan Police, have announced they are no longer prosecuting for possession of small amounts of cannabis. Instead they are issuing warnings (with no apparent record) and disposing of the drug, so saving time to focus on harder or larger-scale dealing. If successful, this project may be implemented in other areas of the city.

This has been regarded as a de facto admission that because of the large numbers of people who regularly flout the cannabis laws, it is a waste of resources to push them through the judicial system. The question is whether a law that is being broken should be enforced more strongly or changed to accommodate what citizens are doing.

Thirdly, there is debate about the international implications of changing the law in one nation. The 1961 UN convention on Narcotic Drugs provides the framework for UK drug laws and it requires each participating nation to legislate against banned substances, this includes cannabis. It is clear that decriminalisation is possible within the convention. Several signatories to the convention have already done this, the Netherlands for example, with moves in this direction also in a number of other European countries such as Belgium, Portugal and Spain. However, it is not yet clear whether legalisation of cannabis would be permissible or would require a nation to opt out of the convention, or at least seek changes to the existing agreement.

Equally significant is the question of whether changes in the law can sensibly be made in one nation, independently of others. This is a particular issue in Europe where the absence of border controls means that any country which relaxes its laws may find itself becoming a focus of drug use and sale and 'drug tourism'. The issue here is whether any change in the law can be unilateral or needs to be multilateral.

Fourthly, there is debate about whether decriminalisation or legalisation would actually reduce or increase drug-related problems. Would they result in a reduction in drug-related crime, removal of the drug trade from large-scale criminal dealers and associated violence and would it be easier for people with drug problems to come forward for help? It is unlikely that changes to the law on cannabis, but not other drugs, would have such positive impacts. On the other hand would liberalising cannabis drug laws result in more people using it and possibly more people having problems with cannabis and other drugs?

Last is the issue of practical details, one which many people who are either for or against law changes seem to ignore. Exactly what changes in the law should be made but also who would produce and sell cannabis, what controls would there be, what about age limits etc.?

Price and product

Bought on the streets, resin costs around £93 per ounce or £15 for an eighth of an ounce. Herbal cannabis costs anything from £60 per ounce to £116 for strong strains such as skunk (source – Independent Drug Monitoring Unit Drug Prices). Heavy and regular cannabis users might use an eighth of an ounce per day. Many people only smoke occasionally.

Recently, stronger types of herbal cannabis have become available with names like northern lights and super skunk. They are grown from specially cultivated seeds, often imported from Holland.

The effects of these strains are more pronounced and can cause hallucinogenic effects. Some people may find them too strong and the experience of smoking them very disturbing, while others may enjoy the greater effects. Increasing amounts of these strains are being homegrown for private use or sold on the cash market and among friends.

■ The above information is from DrugScope's web site which can be found at www.drugscope.org.uk

Cannabis – facts and urban myths

There's a huge amount of information out there about cannabis. It can be difficult to separate out fact from myth – even the media, politicians and police get their facts wrong from time to time.

This article looks at some of the key facts, and the myths about cannabis.

Where does our cannabis come from?

Cannabis grows in most parts of the world. In some countries it literally grows as a weed, and in others it is cultivated as a crop. Some of this is used for industrial purposes: the fibres are used to make cloth, rope and paper. The seeds are used to make oil for paints and cosmetics, and as food for people and animals. And the plants are also cultivated to produce drugs for home consumption and for export.

In the past, most of the UK's cannabis was imported from overseas. We used to get a lot of cannabis from Morocco, Pakistan, India and Afghanistan. Most of this was in the form of cannabis resin (hash) rather than herbal cannabis (weed). Herbal cannabis is also smuggled into the UK; lots of this is grown commercially in the Netherlands, although other countries like South Africa are exporting more herbal cannabis too.

By Kevin Flemen

Over the past few years, there has been a big growth in the UK's homegrown market and this makes up a bigger share of what people use.

What gets used?

The two main products on sale in the UK are herbal cannabis and cannabis resin. Herbal cannabis may

It can be difficult to separate out fact from myth

range from bits and pieces of dried plant material to very strong dried flower buds. Cannabis resin (hash) should be made by collecting the dried resin from plants which is compressed into blocks, but in the UK the product that is usually sold is low-grade 'soap'. The third form, cannabis oil, is rarely sold in the UK.

Is cannabis stronger now than it was twenty years ago?

There are lots of compounds in cannabis and these give the plant its psychoactive properties. One of the most important of these is a chemical called THC. The flowering parts of the female plant have the highest concentration of THC.

So how many people use cannabis in the UK?

According to the *British Crime Survey*, just under 25% of 16- to 19-year-olds reported cannabis use in the last year. 15% of people in this age group said that they had used in the last month. So even though the impression from the media is that the majority of young people are using cannabis, this is not what the research says. The figures for all the age groups in the survey are in the table below.

Cannabis	16-19	10-24	25-34	34-59	16-59
Last Year %	24.6	27.2	14.9	4.3	10.9
Last Month %	15.3	17.1	9.4	2.5	6.7

Source: British Crime Survey 2002-3

By selectively breeding plants, growers have cultivated strains of cannabis that can have very high levels of THC. Some of these strains include 'skunk', 'white widow', 'northern lights', and 'Purple Haze'. There are many other strains too. The THC content of some of these plants can be as much as 20%. Low-grade herbal cannabis can be as low as 1%-2%, so these cultivated strains are much stronger.

On the other hand, lots of cannabis resin in the UK used to be very strong. High-quality hash – which should be resin from the flowers and no plant material – was as strong as much of the new strains of cannabis.

Cannabis and health

Arguments about cannabis seem to fall into two camps: some people are determined that it is harmless and others say it is very dangerous. The truth seems to fall somewhere between these two extremes.

Smoking cannabis

Smoking cannabis is bad for your lungs. If it is smoked in spliffs with tobacco and a cardboard roach instead of a filter, large quantities of soot, tar and other toxins are taken deep into the lungs. The British Lung Foundation suggested that smoking three spliffs a day was the equivalent to smoking twenty cigarettes.

Smoking cannabis in pipes is also bad for the lungs: it still means that lots of toxins reach the lungs. While some products like water pipes reduce some of the risks, they do not make smoking safe – just a bit less damaging.

Cannabis and mental health

The impact on mental wellbeing is one of the biggest concerns about cannabis. Some experts are concerned that cannabis use can cause a range of mental health problems. This could range from problems with concentration, depression or worse symptoms such as paranoia and panic attacks. For most people these symptoms will go away when the person reduces their cannabis use. A smaller number of people go on to develop more serious psychiatric

---

Arguments about cannabis seem to fall into two camps: some people are determined that it is harmless and others say it is very dangerous

---

illnesses such as schizophrenia. There doesn't seem to be any clear pattern as to who is at risk. But people who smoke heavily, people who are prone to panic attacks or depression or have a family history of mental illness, or people who are smoking lots of strong cannabis seem to be most at risk.

Cannabis as a medicine

Some people have claimed that cannabis can be used to treat a range of ailments including nausea, glaucoma, pain, muscular spasms and other problems.

The UK Government licensed trials of cannabis and one company has been cultivating cannabis under licence for these trials. The trials have been partially successful and it seems likely that some cannabis medicines will be on the market in the next few years. But GPs cannot, at present, prescribe cannabis in the UK, and it is not legal for people not involved in the trials to use it.

The reclassification of cannabis

Cannabis is still illegal! In January 2004, cannabis was moved from class

B to class C. However, it remains illegal to possess, grow, supply cannabis or to allow it to be smoked on your premises.

The Association of Chief Police Officers (ACPO) has issued guidance to police forces to say that, in most situations, police officers should not arrest people for possession of cannabis; instead they should confiscate the drug and give the person a warning.

However, the police will still have the power to arrest people for possession of cannabis and have been told to arrest people if they are:

- Under 18
- Using in a public place or around young people
- Are 'known' to the police for cannabis offences or
- Where there are concerns about public disorder.
- Police will also arrest where they suspect supply is taking place.

For people under 18, possession of cannabis may result in a reprimand if it is a first offence. But if a person has already had a reprimand, they may be referred to a Youth Offending Team (YOT) or go to court. This would result in a criminal record which could affect job prospects and travel. Schools can still exclude pupils for being involved with cannabis at school. So even though cannabis has been reclassified, everyone still needs to be aware of the legal issues and health risks that can result from using it.

What's in 'soap'?

Most high quality cannabis resin never gets to the UK. Instead the main form of resin sold in the UK is 'soap bar'. This is often a low-grade mixture of chopped plant, resin, colourant and other additives. Some sources say that soap-bar may have other additives – paraffin wax, henna, glues and other drugs have reportedly been mixed into soap-bar.

- This document was written by Kevin Flemen, KFx Drugs Awareness: www.ixion.demon.co.uk The web site is suitable for school-age pupils and no unacceptable links are included on the site.

© Kevin Flemen, KFx Drugs Awareness

Cannabis economy brings in £11bn

Cannabis smokers just want to stay on the sofa and snack, spending hours engrossed in home entertainment. Red Bull and smoothies, 'munchie' snacks such as Mars bars and Haribo jellies. Pizza chains. Video stores. Games consoles. Multichannel TV. And what scares them . . . Shiny, noisy places with too many choices such as Starbucks and McDonald's. High-alcohol drinks and strong lagers such as Stella Artois. Pubs with bouncers on the door: Businesses alerted to huge profits as study shows dope users have money to burn

By Ben Summerskill

The stock market is faltering and house prices are on the edge of a precipice. Could cannabis smokers be the unlikely saviours of the British economy?

A major new study is being used to advise well-known household and high-street companies about the gains and losses they face as cannabis smoking becomes commonplace.

Research has revealed that Britain's 'cannabis economy' is worth £5 billion a year in sales alone.

Now it has been discovered that a further £6bn of consumer expenditure each year is closely linked to the growing cannabis-users' market.

'Young people between 15 and 30 are very trend-conscious and aspirational,' said Andy Davidson, who commissioned the study for The Research Business International, trend analysts who tracked the spending habits of young people for six months. The study found that cannabis users spend an average of £20 on products that accompany their drug use each time they smoke.

> *Because smoking cannabis heightens appetite, users are providing a £120 million weekly windfall to a string of takeaway food suppliers*

Because smoking cannabis heightens appetite, users are providing a £120 million weekly windfall to a string of takeaway food suppliers, such as Domino and Pizza Hut, and manufacturers of 'munchie' products such as Mars bars and Haribo jellies.

Video suppliers and manufacturers of home entertainments such as PlayStation and Nintendo GameCube are also benefiting from the need of a generation of users to keep themselves occupied at home while their drug of choice remains unlawful.

'Some of these brands benefit at the moment,' said Davidson, 'but if people become more willing to smoke in public when the law is relaxed next year, they may be hit.'

The Government has announced that cannabis will be 'downgraded' to a class C drug next summer making arrest and prosecution for possession less likely. The move follows a controversial experiment in Lambeth, south London, where police attention focused on hard drug users and suppliers rather than cannabis smokers.

'Cannabis users also have discretionary expenditure of tens of millions of pounds each week on places to meet and eat,' said Davidson. 'They don't like shiny, noisy

MUNCHIES & CO INDUSTRIES

Profits

Proud makers of Lard Pizza & Chokko Bar

environments with lots of choices such as McDonald's. On the whole, they prefer somewhere with low-key lighting and a straightforward menu.

'And they don't like venues solely devoted to heavy drinking. That doesn't mean that they won't still go out for a big night once a week, but they avoid the sort of pubs that have heavy bouncers on the door.' Many cannabis users also avoid high alcohol drinks, even strong lagers.

'Thursday is now my biggest night,' reported a 22-year old woman from London. 'I hate Saturday, it's full of idiots, it's expensive. That's when I love to stay at home and smoke [cannabis].'

'I don't visit big chain bars any more,' said Anthony Green, a student from Leicester. 'They're very intolerant of anything that's outside their obvious remit of drinking and pulling.

'When we use cannabis at home, there are some things we always consume at the same time. Red Bull or smoothies, for example, and takeaway food. There's a sort of conspiracy between consumers and retailers nowadays. You know why you buy these things and they know why you're buying these things, but no one says anything.'

Drug use may even affect radio and TV scheduling in future, the research suggests. A typical 24-year-old male admitted: 'I've started taking much more interest in the Discovery Channel. Cannabis really gets you thinking deeply about things.'

There are six million regular users, more people than attend church, play Sunday league football or go jogging

---

Government research has already confirmed that more than 15 million people in Britain have tried cannabis. There are six million regular users, more people than attend church, play Sunday league football or go jogging. TRBI's Project Edge is the first study which has openly monitored cannabis use for commercial, rather than medical, purposes.

Tobacco companies have worked secretly for years on trials of cannabis cigarettes, in spite of the fact that their scientists working on the projects risk arrest for drug possession.

However, manufacturers such as Imperial Tobacco still insist that their 'King Size' Rizla cigarette papers are intended solely for making handmade cigarettes rather than rolling joints.

Carl Ratcliff of advertising agency TBWA said: 'As cannabis gets closer to decriminalisation, you'll see more brands recognising that through their advertising. It won't be explicit, but will be heavily implicit in terms of the signs and symbols that they use.'

'It's no longer a moral issue,' said Davidson. 'Businesses targeting the youth market can no longer ignore the fact that almost half of their customer base is getting stoned every day. They need to make specific projections about how that affects them.'

■ This article first appeared in *The Observer*, 2 February 2003.
© Guardian Newspapers Limited 2003

Cannabis misconceptions

Information from DrugScope

Does cannabis lead people to use hard drugs?
There are two theories that have become 'common currency' as understandings in relation to this question. While they actually propose different things, they are often misunderstood as being the same and are therefore mistakenly used interchangeably. To briefly outline the differences between the two, the stepping-stone theory suggests that progression from so-called 'soft' drugs such as cannabis to so-called 'hard' drugs like heroin is progressive and inevitable. The gateway theory draws on the metaphor of a series of gates through which an individual may pass. Each gateway leads to a different drug and new risks. In contrast to the stepping-stone theory, the gateway theory does

not propose an inevitable progression, but does propose the possibility of using various drugs.

In reality, the gateway theory seems to be far more credible. While it is certainly true that many of those who become heroin addicts, for example, have used cannabis, the vast majority of people in the UK (and elsewhere) who have used cannabis, have never used so-called harder drugs such as heroin or cocaine. This would suggest that progression from cannabis to so-called 'harder' drugs is in no way inevitable, in fact it is relatively rare.

Recent research by the Home Office also concluded that 'the association between harmful and less harmful drugs found in survey data is spurious' and that the gateway effects are probably 'very small'.

Is cannabis a soft drug?
Drugs are very often spoken about in terms of two broad categories – 'hard' and 'soft' drugs. So-called 'hard' drugs, such as heroin, cocaine and 'crack' cocaine, are described as 'hard' because they are associated with a number of potential dangers, such as addiction or other health risks including death. So-called 'soft' drugs are described as such because they are generally believed to entail a lesser degree of risk. These categories are, however, part of the misleading discourse on illicit drugs, as they do

not stand up to examination. Many over-the-counter and prescribed drugs are addictive, carry significant side-effects and result in numerous fatalities each year. Likewise, both alcohol and tobacco, not considered to be 'drugs' at all by some, carry health risks and mortality rates that far exceed many illicit drugs including some of the 'harder' ones. Certainly some drugs are more harmful than others, but hard/soft terminology does not adequately or appropriately demonstrate this.

One consequence of the 'hard'-'soft' dichotomy is that so-called 'soft' drugs may be seen as harmless in relation to the perceived risks of 'hard' drugs. Yet the use of 'soft' drugs, e.g. ecstasy, has been associated with a number of deaths in recent years (though the cause of such deaths is frequently misunderstood). The logic of the 'hard'-'soft' dichotomy also suggests that legal substances – alcohol and tobacco – must be even less risky than so-called 'soft' drugs. Again, this is simply not true. It has been estimated that cigarettes alone account for well over 100,000 premature deaths per year in Britain. Alcohol is thought to cause around 28,000 excess deaths per year in England and Wales and 2,000,000 deaths per year worldwide. It is also the case that what are regarded as 'hard' and 'soft' drugs change according to time and place. In the 1950s, cannabis was associated with addiction and violence. Few people would associate this drug with such qualities today.

Is cannabis harmless?

Cannabis is considered to be a 'soft' drug by most people and, apart perhaps from the mistaken belief that it will lead to 'hard' drug use, it is seen by many as a fairly benign drug. However, this does not mean that the use of cannabis entails no health-risks.

It has been argued that cannabis smoke contains carcinogenic substances. The British Lung Foundation recently reported that smoking 3 cannabis 'joints' was equivalent to 20 cigarettes. When cannabis is smoked mixed with tobacco, the problems associated with tobacco smoking also become relevant.

> *One consequence of the 'hard'-'soft' dichotomy is that so-called 'soft' drugs may be seen as harmless in relation to the perceived risks of 'hard' drugs*

Cannabis smoking is also believed by some experts to be associated with conditions such as bronchitis. The point here is that as soon as you start to burn something and inhale that smoke a range of health risks are created. Evidence about cannabis's relative harm in this respect (compared to say cigarettes) is as yet contradictory.

Some experts believe that cannabis use must also be seen as involving some risk of dependence. It is clear however that while some individuals may suffer from problems not dissimilar in many ways to a dependence syndrome, for the majority of users dependence is not an outcome and as such cannabis would not normatively be understood as a drug of addiction. In considering this issue, it is important to understand that dependence must be seen within the context of the drug in question, the individual in question and their social context. Dependence is, therefore, a relationship and is not simply a property of any given substance. Some drugs (heroin, cocaine, alcohol, tobacco) are more addictive than others – cannabis is less so.

One further issue pertaining to cannabis and the question of harm, relates to individuals with mental health issues. Although the evidence is not conclusive, some research has suggested that cannabis can stimulate mental health disorders such as schizophrenia. Put briefly, any 'mind altering substances' may involve additional problems for those with mental health problems.

References

Pudney, S. (2002) *The road to ruin? Sequences of initiation into drug use and offending by young people and Britain.* Home Office.

■ The above information is from DrugScope's web site which can be found at www.drugscope.org.uk

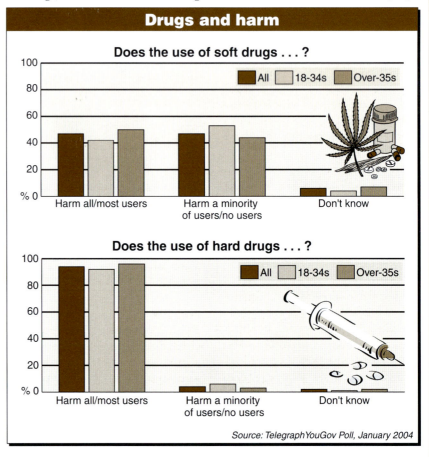

Drugs and harm

Does the use of soft drugs . . . ?

Does the use of hard drugs . . . ?

Source: Telegraph YouGov Poll, January 2004

The cannabis market

British teenagers use so much cannabis that market is saturated, says EU report

Cannabis use among teenagers in the UK has begun to stabilise, but only because it is so widespread the market has become saturated, the European Union's drug agency warned yesterday.

The EU monitoring centre on drugs and drug abuse also warned of new public health dangers from the increasing potency of cannabis available in Britain. It raised concerns about the long-term health implications of the emergence of a significant new group of teenage boys who are using cannabis intensively – more than 20 times a month.

Its annual report, published in October 2003, says the official goal of reducing drug consumption by 2006 across Europe remains a long way off, with at least one in five adults in the EU having tried cannabis and an emerging problem of growing cocaine use in some cities, particularly in Britain.

The agency warns that the drug-related death toll continues to rise – there are between 7,000 and 9,000 deaths every year in the EU.

It says that glue-sniffing and other forms of solvent abuse have proved a much greater acute health risk for young people in the UK than ecstasy, which causes fewer but more highly publicised deaths.

It says that there were 1,700 deaths from solvent abuse in the UK between 1983 and 2000, with most of the victims aged 16 to 19 – far more than the 'relatively rare' ecstasy deaths.

The authors say that recent government measures have been effective in sharply reducing solvent-abuse deaths in Britain over the last four years.

Solvents remain the third most commonly used drug after cannabis and alcohol, with 15% of 15- and 16-year-olds trying them at some time.

The EU says that ecstasy use was high in 1995 in the UK, Italy and Ireland but has recently seen some decline. It suggests that the

By Alan Travis in Strasbourg

high-profile negative media coverage has been a factor.

The report also confirms the more liberal approach of many governments to drug policy, with harm-reduction measures such as needle exchanges, drug consumption rooms, methadone treatment, heroin prescribing and pill testing becoming an established part of health policy in Holland, Germany and Spain.

However, it shows that the UK is lagging behind other European countries in providing treatment places for hardcore drug abusers.

> *The UK has one of the highest usage levels in Europe, with 42% of all 15- to 34-year-olds saying they had tried it at least once – second only to Denmark*

But while Switzerland is about to become the first country to legalise cannabis possession, the eastern European states which are to join the EU next May have been busy outlawing it for the first time.

Georges Estievenart, director of the agency, said there were some grounds for cautious optimism about the drug situation in Europe, such as the adoption of a drug strategy by most national governments.

But he added that this was outweighed by the fact that the overall drug use trend remained upward and there was 'insufficient impact on regular drug use by a worrying number of young people in EU countries'.

The report says that cannabis remains the illicit drug most frequently used by young people across

Europe. The UK has one of the highest usage levels in Europe, with 42% of all 15- to 34-year-olds saying they had tried it at least once – second only to Denmark.

The price of cannabis resin has been stable across the rest of Europe but has fallen sharply in the past four years in Britain, possibly as a result of the rapid rise in homegrown marijuana production, which has been estimated at 50% of the market. Hashish, which is nearly all imported from Morocco, is cheapest in Britain at €2.3 (£1.60) a gram, and most expensive in Norway at €26.6.

'Europe remains the world's biggest market for cannabis resin (hashish), accounting for some three-quarters of global seizures. Herbal cannabis or marijuana grown in the EU is also becoming increasingly available.

'Evidence indicates that the average potency of cannabis in the EU has risen and now ranges from around 5-10% for both resin and herbal varieties, but some samples are considerably stronger with a THC [the active ingredient] content of up to 30%. This raises public health concerns.'

A decade ago the THC content of most cannabis was about 1% to 2%.

But the EU's drugs agency is also worried about the emergence of a new generation of teenage boys who are starting to use cannabis at a younger age, instead of sniffing glue. They are using it more intensively – more than 20 times a month – and persist with it perhaps until their early 20s. It says this pattern of use is often mixed with binge drinking.

The report for the first time looks at the drug situation in eastern Europe and warns that some countries, including Estonia and Latvia, will be facing 'the most rapidly developing HIV epidemic in the world' unless syringe and needle exchange programmes are adopted to tackle the problem.

© *Guardian Newspapers Limited 2003*

Cannabis – the lies and the truth

Information from the Coalition Against Cannabis

The lie
It is claimed that smoking cannabis is a harmless activity, posing little or no danger.

The truth
Cannabis is a toxic substance, dangerous to health and society.

The lie
It is claimed that cannabis has no long-term effects.

The truth
Cancers of the lung, head and neck have been reported in young individuals. Schizophrenia can be triggered and permanent brain damage is a distinct possibility.

The lie
It is claimed that cannabis is no more dangerous than tobacco.

The truth
Cannabis contains more carcinogens than tobacco, and deposits four times as much tar in the airways and lungs. Smoking 3-4 joints causes as much damage as 20 cigarettes.

The lie
It is claimed that cannabis smoking does not lead to the use of other drugs.

The truth
Using cannabis just once a week can make a person sixty times more likely to progress to other illicit drugs.

The lie
It is claimed that cannabis is not addictive.

The truth
Cannabis can produce both physical and psychological dependence. Of six million drug addicts currently in America, sixty per cent are dependent on cannabis.

The lie
It is claimed that the effects of cannabis wear off quickly.

The truth
Cannabis is fat-soluble, so stays in the body for several weeks, unlike alcohol. Driving is affected for at least twenty-four hours. On just one joint a month, learning and memory are constantly impaired.

The lie
It is claimed that cannabis is helpful to those who are tense, exhausted or depressed.

The truth
Recent research has again confirmed that cannabis is associated with anxiety, depression, suicidal behaviour and psychosis including schizophrenia.

The lie
It is claimed that cannabis is not really harmful to young people.

The truth
Concentration, attention span, learning and memory are all severely affected. Few children, using cannabis even occasionally, will achieve their full potential.

The lie
It is claimed that people should be allowed to experiment with drugs, it is their own personal affair.

The truth
No drug is victimless. Cannabis is implicated in an increasing number of road accidents. Addicts and those suffering from psychosis and schizophrenia need NHS treatment at the taxpayer's expense. Harm from passive smoking does occur.

The lie
It is claimed that people who used it in the 1960s are absolutely fine.

The truth
Cannabis is now at least ten times stronger than in the sixties. Today's cannabis is a very different drug to cannabis in the 1960s.

The lie
It is claimed that cannabis use is a harmless pastime of the young, they get it from friends and siblings.

The truth
It is an industry, totally controlled by violent criminal gangs, operating a nationwide network of distributing and selling of other illicit drugs.

The lie
It is claimed that cannabis is desperately needed for medicine.

The truth
Medicines have to be pure single substances. Cannabis contains four hundred chemicals. Pure THC from cannabis, already available as nabilone, is not so effective as other current medicine for many conditions.

■ The above information is from the National Coalition Against Cannabis.

© Maranatha Community, a member of the National Coalition Against Cannabis

Cannabis – a soft drug?

By Prof. Les Iversen
PhD, FRS

After tobacco and alcohol, cannabis is one of the most widely used of all 'recreational' drugs. In Britain and the USA nearly half of all 18-year-olds admit to having tried the drug and 10-20% of 16- 24-year-olds are current users. Because the active ingredient in herbal cannabis, delta-9-tetrahydrocannabinol (THC), is poorly absorbed when taken orally and is too insoluble to inject, the drug is most commonly administered by smoking. THC acts on specific receptors on the surface of some brain cells; these receptors are normally activated by anandamide and related chemicals made naturally in the brain as part of a chemical signalling system.

THC has complex effects on brain function. It affects movement and balance control, distorts the sense of time, reduces sensitivity to pain and increases appetite. Users take the drug for the pleasant feelings of relaxation, social ease and the state of heightened perception and euphoria which accompany the cannabis 'high'.

There is a large literature on the effects of cannabis in human subjects (reviewed by Hollister, 1986, 1998; Iversen, 2000, 2002). The acute effects of the drug are relatively benign. There are virtually no cases of death from overdose, and cannabis intoxication is usually not accompanied by the increased aggression and violence often associated with alcohol. As with other intoxicants, driving under the influence of cannabis is not recommended – although the impairments measured in driving-simulators are relatively modest.

The chronic use of cannabis, however, carries some more serious hazards – although these tend to have been exaggerated in the official messages currently conveyed to young people. Possibly the most serious risk is related to the fact that the drug is commonly administered by smoking – often in the UK in combination with tobacco. Cannabis smoke contains many of the same noxious chemicals present in tobacco smoke, and it causes lung irritation which can lead to bronchitis. There is as yet no evidence for an increased risk of lung cancer in cannabis users, although some small-scale clinical studies have suggested an increased risk of cancers of the mouth and throat. Regular cannabis users may become dependent on the drug, and they may seek treatment to break their habit. It has been estimated that approximately 10% of those who use cannabis become dependent. On the other hand, the majority of cannabis users quit before the age of 30.

Earlier alarms about the alleged ill-effects of cannabis on reproductive function, the immune system and the so-called 'amotivational state' have proved unfounded, as have claims that the drug can cause permanent brain damage. Controversy remains about the relationship between cannabis use and psychiatric illness. Whilst cannabis tends to exacerbate the symptoms of those already suffering such illnesses, the evidence that cannabis may actually provoke long-term psychiatric breakdown is far less clear (Iversen, 2002).

Summary

Cannabis

- Cannabis acts on brain receptors that normally recognise the natural cannabinoid chemical anandamide.
- The active compound in cannabis, tetrahydrocannabinol (THC), cannot be injected and is most efficiently delivered to the brain by smoking.
- Cannabis is safe in overdose, and intoxication does not lead to violent behaviour.
- Smoking cannabis carries hazards of bronchitis and other lung diseases, including possibly cancer – although there is at yet no evidence for the latter.
- There is little evidence that long-term cannabis use damages the brain, immune system or reproductive function, but it can make psychiatric illness worse.
- Approximately 10% of regular cannabis users become dependent, and some may seek treatment.

Stages of cannabis intoxication

Buzz – dizziness, light-headed, tingling, warmth
High – heightened perception, giggly, euphoria, rush of thoughts and ideas
Stoned – relaxed, peaceful, calm, distorted sense of time, maybe hallucinations, fantasies
Sleep

■ Prof Iversen is Visiting Professor, University of Oxford, and Director of the Wolfson Centre for Age-Related Diseases at King's College, University of London.

■ The above information is from a Beckley Foundation seminar: Drugs and the Brain, held at Magdalen College, Oxford, 2002. For further information visit their web site at www.beckleyfoundation.co.uk

Cannabis and mental health

Information from Rethink

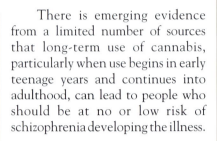

rethink
severe mental illness

Introduction

Rethink, formerly known as the National Schizophrenia Fellowship, is the charity for people who experience severe mental illness and for those who care for them. We are both a campaigning membership charity, with a network of mutual support groups around the country, and a large voluntary sector provider in mental health, helping 7,500 people each day. Through all its work, Rethink aims to help people who experience severe mental illness to achieve a meaningful and fulfilling life and to press for their families and friends to obtain the support they need.

On 29 January, cannabis was be reclassified by the Home Office from a Class B to a Class C drug. The change is being accompanied by a £1 million awareness campaign organised from the Home Office that emphasises that cannabis will remain an illegal drug. The awareness campaign does not highlight the mental health dangers associated with cannabis use.

What are the mental health dangers?

There is a general consensus that use of cannabis by someone who has schizophrenia worsens the psychotic symptoms of the illness – paranoia, hallucinations and delusions. This is also true for people with bipolar affective disorder (manic depression) experiencing psychotic symptoms.

There is strong evidence from a wide range of sources that long-term and short-term use of cannabis can 'trigger' a psychotic episode or schizophrenia in people who are at high risk of developing schizophrenia – for instance, people who have close family members who have schizophrenia.

> ### Summary
>
> Cannabis was reclassified on 29 January 2004 from a Class B to a Class C drug.
>
> Rethink severe mental illness is concerned that:
> - the mental health risks associated with cannabis are not widely understood
> - the government's publicity campaign does not highlight these mental health risks
> - more resources need to be put into mental health warnings on the use of cannabis.

There is emerging evidence from a limited number of sources that long-term use of cannabis, particularly when use begins in early teenage years and continues into adulthood, can lead to people who should be at no or low risk of schizophrenia developing the illness.

What is being done about this?

The Home Office awareness campaign, which includes a four-week-long radio campaigning beginning on 24 January, a range of leaflets and posters aimed at young people, concentrates on the message 'Cannabis is still illegal.' None of the material we have seen mentions the impact of cannabis on mental health.

In late February, a health campaign organised by the Home Office will target 13- 18-year-olds with a range of messages that will mention mental health, but only in passing. It is understood that just £50,000 of the £1 million total is being spent on general health-awareness messages.

What should be done about this?

Rethink believes that young people are hearing that, as a result of this reclassification, cannabis is no longer regarded as a serious drug and that the police won't make arrests except in the most serious circumstances. Young people are getting the message that cannabis is risk-free.

A long-term, well-funded, innovative campaign aimed at publicising the real mental health risks associated with cannabis needs to be in place as soon as possible to counter this 'risk-free' message.

■ The above information is from Rethink's web site which can be found at www.rethink.org

© Rethink

Cannabis-related harms on health

Information from DrugScope

Cannabis is the most widely used illicit drug, and has been used by a substantial minority of young adults in many western societies. This is despite the evidence that cannabis may be associated with a number of harms. However, in assessing this evidence for the effects of cannabis it should be borne in mind that:

- some of the harms are the result of cannabis smoke rather than cannabis itself
- it is difficult to distinguish between the effects of tobacco and cannabis which are often used together by cannabis users
- there is a lack of controlled long-term studies that makes many conclusions tentative
- the difficulty in determining the amount of tetrahydrocannabinol (THC), the main active constituent of cannabis, consumed by most users cannabis-using careers are time-limited and most users stop their cannabis use in their mid to late twenties.

Acute effects

- Anxiety and panic especially in inexperienced users
- impaired attention, memory and psychomotor performance while intoxicated
- increased risk of accident if an intoxicated person drives a car or operates machinery, particularly if cannabis is combined with alcohol use
- increased risk of psychotic symptoms among those who are vulnerable because of a personal or family history of psychosis.

Chronic effects

- Cannabis can probably cause bronchitis and histapathological changes
- there may be a dependence syndrome associated with cannabis, marked by an inability to abstain or control cannabis use
- subtle impairments of attention and memory that persist while the user is chronically intoxicated that may or may not be reversible after prolonged abstinence
- cannabis is possibly linked with increased risk of cancers of the oral cavity, pharynx and oesophagus
- cannabis is possibly linked with impaired educational attainment

There may be a dependence syndrome associated with cannabis, marked by an inability to abstain or control cannabis use

in adolescents and under-achievement in adults in jobs requiring a high level of cognitive skills.

Harms that may be experienced by particular sub-populations

- Those whose cannabis use starts in early teens are at increased risk of using other illicit drugs
- women who continue to use cannabis during pregnancy are at risk of producing low-birthweight babies
- cannabis may exacerbate the illnesses of those suffering from emphysema, bronchitis, schizophrenia and alcohol and other drug dependencies.

- The above information is from DrugScope. See page 41 for their address details.

© *DrugScope*

Addiction

Which of these drugs are seriously addictive?

	All	18-34s	Over 35s
Heroin	96%	96%	96%
Crack cocaine	94%	93%	95%
Tobacco	92%	93%	92%
Alcohol	75%	77%	74%
Amphetamines	61%	55%	64%
Coffee	46%	58%	40%
LSD	46%	33%	52%
Cannabis	44%	38%	48%
Ecstasy	39%	32%	43%

Source: Telegraph YouGov Poll, January 2004

Cannabis deaths

Cannabis use causes 'hundreds of deaths a year', coroner warns

By Julie Henry,
Education Correspondent

Britain's most senior coroner is warning that hundreds of young people are dying in accidents caused by their prolonged use of cannabis.

Hamish Turner, the president of the Coroners' Society, said that the drug, which is often portrayed as harmless, has increasingly been behind deaths that have been recorded as accidents or suicides.

In the past year, he estimated that cannabis was a significant contributory factor in about 10 per cent of the 100 cases that he had dealt with in south Devon, where he works.

Conversations with his colleagues led him to believe that the scale of the problem elsewhere in the country was equally bad. 'Cannabis is as dangerous as any other drug and people must understand that it kills,' said Mr Turner.

'From my long experience I can say that it is a very dangerous substance. Increasingly it is mentioned not only as the first drug taken by people who overdose, but also in suicides and accidental deaths.

'It is an awful waste of young lives. People are trying the drug at a very young age. Many go on to harder drugs and I am dealing with more and more heroin overdoses. People can also suffer severe consequences from the cannabis alone, however.

'Bereaved parents say to me, "We didn't realise how dangerous it was until it was too late, if only we had done something". It is heartbreaking.'

Recent examples of the dangers of the drug cited by Mr Turner include the case of James Taylor, a 31-year-old, who was found hanged in his Torquay flat. The inquest heard that he had started smoking cannabis when he was about 15 and was a habitual user. The drug was blamed for the depression and mental health problems that later plagued him and which led to his death.

Mary Taylor, his mother, said that there was no doubt in her mind that cannabis had killed her son. 'The cannabis made him paranoid from the word go. He went from a good-looking, artistic, talented chap to someone who did not trust anyone, not even his sister, who he was very close to.

'Because of the damage the drug did to him he became more isolated, more lonely and more depressed. The loveliest boy was destroyed by this drug. I would never have believed that James would have acted as he did when he took his own life.

'People who insist that cannabis is harmless are talking rubbish. We had years of hell when James was on cannabis, and that was all he was taking. Now he is dead and our family life has been devastated.'

Cannabis also contributed to the death of Dragan Radoslavjevic, 42, from Paignton, Devon. He died earlier this year after using a power tool to drill a hole in his head. An inquest in Torquay heard that he suffered from depression and relied on drugs such as cannabis and heroin.

Mr Turner said that stronger varieties of cannabis – up to 10 times more potent than those used in the 1960s – were now common, leading to physical and mental problems in young people living in rural areas as well as in cities.

The drug robbed young people of their appetite for life, the coroner warned, with regular and prolonged use leading to panic attacks, paranoia, psychosis, racing heart, agitation, an increased risk of heart attacks and strokes, and even a tendency to violence.

'Cannabis is a mind-altering drug which has ravaging effects on the brain,' he added.

In another case, Ralph Hamilton, 27, from Torquay, died when the car he was driving hit a bus in Totnes. Witnesses reported that he 'looked almost comatose' as he drove directly into the front of the open-topped bus. Blood tests showed that Mr Hamilton had been taking cannabis and the inquest heard that he was a regular user.

Other coroners also expressed concern about cannabis. Michael Gwynne, the coroner for Telford and Wrekin, said that he feared that deaths would spiral if the Government decriminalised the drug. 'There is clearly some evidence that cannabis is a contributory factor in

Drug-related poisoning deaths

By selected type of drug[1]

England and Wales					Numbers
	1993	1995	1998	1999	2000
Heroin and morphine[2]	187	357	646	754	926
Paracetamol[3]	463	526	523	473	455
Antidepressants	461	489	510	493	449
Methadone	232	310	364	298	238
Temazepam	173	138	111	82	73
Cocaine	12	19	66	88	80
Barbiturates	44	46	35	26	17
MDMA/Ecstasy	8	10	16	26	36
Cannabis	14	17	5	8	11
All drug-related deaths[4]	2,252	2,563	2,922	2,943	2,968

1 Where more than one drug is mentioned on the death certificate the death is included in the figures for each drug. In these cases it is not possible to determine which drug was primarily responsible for the death.

2 As heroin breaks down in the body into morphine, the latter may be detected at post mortem and recorded on the death certificate.

3 Includes deaths with any mention of paracetamol or any compounds containing paracetamol.

4 Includes deaths related to all other drugs.

Source: Social Trends No. 33: 2003 edition. Office for National Statistics, Crown copyright

drug-related traffic accident deaths but, because of the problems with toxicology, we are unable to state its full impact,' he said.

'What the Government should not do is become more tolerant of the drug; that would involve setting legal limits, and risk cannabis becoming a major cause of road traffic deaths.'

Veronica Hamilton-Deely, the Brighton and Hove coroner, said that national figures supplied by coroners' offices showed that illicit drugs, particularly cannabis, were increasingly present in victims of road traffic fatalities. These statistics showed that in 2000, 12 per cent of

the 3,400 people killed in road accidents showed traces of cannabis: a sixfold increase on a decade earlier.

The dangers of cannabis were highlighted in research published in June 2003, which showed a sharp increase in drug-related deaths. According to the European Centre for Addiction Studies at St George's Hospital Medical School in London, in 2002, British coroners cited cannabis as the major cause of death in 18 out of 853 drug-related deaths. The drug was also implicated in a further 31 out of 1,579 deaths involving a cocktail of drugs.

The biggest killers were heroin, which was the major cause of death in 712 cases, and cocaine, which was the principal factor in 147 deaths.
© Telegraph Group Limited, London 2004

Cannabis link to psychosis

Very heavy use of cannabis could be a cause of psychosis, according to a leading psychiatrist who believes that society should think carefully about the potential consequences of its increasing use.

Robin Murray, professor of psychiatry at the Institute of Psychiatry and consultant psychiatrist at the Maudsley hospital in London, says that in the last 18 months, there has been increasing evidence that cannabis causes serious mental illness. In particular, a Dutch study of 4,000 people from the general population found that those taking large amounts of cannabis were almost seven times more likely to have psychotic symptoms three years later.

'This research must not be ignored,' said Prof Murray, speaking at the annual general meeting of the Royal College of Psychiatrists in Edinburgh.

Writing in the *Guardian* last August, Prof Murray said he had been surprised that the discussion around cannabis had skirted around the issue of psychosis.

Psychiatrists had known for 150 years that very heavy consumption of cannabis could cause hallucinations and delusions.

'This was thought to be very rare and transient until the 1980s

*By Sarah Boseley,
Health Editor*

when, as cannabis consumption rose across Europe and the USA, it became apparent that people with chronic psychotic illnesses were more likely to be regular daily consumers of cannabis than the general population.'

Psychiatrists had known for 150 years that very heavy consumption of cannabis could cause hallucinations and delusions

In the UK, he said, people with schizophrenia are about twice as likely to smoke cannabis. The reason appears to be the effect that the drugs have on chemicals in the brain. 'In schizophrenia, the hallucinations and delusions result from an excess of a brain chemical called dopamine. All the drugs which are known to cause psychosis – amphetamine, cocaine and cannabis – increase the release of dopamine in the brain.'

Cannabis had been the downfall of many a promising student, he suggested. 'Like any practising psychiatrist, I have often listened to the distraught parents of a young man diagnosed with schizophrenia tell me that as a child their son was very bright and had no obvious psychological problems. Then in his mid-teens his grades began falling. He started complaining that his friends were against him and that people were talking about him behind his back.

'After several years of increasingly bizarre behaviour, he dropped out of school, job or university; he was admitted to a psychiatric unit overwhelmed by paranoid fears and persecution by voices. The parents tell me that, at some point, their son was heavily dependent on cannabis.'

It used to be thought that the high numbers of psychotic patients taking cannabis could be explained because they used it to alleviate their symptoms. The recent studies, however, have looked at large populations without mental illness and studied the numbers of cannabis takers within them who have developed psychosis.
© Guardian Newspapers Limited 2003

Cannabis for the GP

Information from the Maranatha Community

On 29 January 2004, cannabis was downgraded from a Class B to a Class C drug. There has been a lot of controversy surrounding the reclassification. What do GPs need to know about the adverse effects of cannabis to advise patients?

Prevalence

The 2001/2002 *British Crime Survey*, published by the Home Office, estimated that over three million of the adult population have used cannabis in past 12 months and two million have used it in the past month. 27% of 16- to 24-year-olds have used cannabis in the last year, 17% have used it in the last month. These are the highest prevalence rates of any European country. Cannabis is easily available: 68% of young people state it is 'very easy' or 'fairly easy' to get cannabis. The mean age of onset of cannabis abuse is 15 years.

The cannabis market

It is estimated that Britain's 'cannabis economy' is worth £5 billion a year with a further £6 billion of consumer expenditure linked to cannabis market due to 'the munchies'.

Constituents of cannabis

Cannabis contains over 400 chemicals, about 60 of which are cannabinoids (compounds with a chemical structure related to delta 9-tetrahydrocannabinol THC, the main active chemical). In terms of potency, it is reported that cannabis has become markedly stronger over the last 20-30 years, with an increase from about 0.5% of THC to 5%, while specially grown varieties may contain up to 30% THC. A reefer in the early 1980s contained about 10mg of THC, whereas a modern 'joint' may contain around 300mg of THC.

The way cannabis is consumed

Cannabis can be eaten (usually baked into cakes/cookies). It is more

the maranatha community

commonly smoked. Compared to tobacco smoking, cannabis smoking is associated with a nearly fivefold greater increment in the blood carboxyhemoglobin level, an approximately threefold increase in the amount of tar inhaled, and retention in the respiratory tract of one-third more inhaled tar. The smoke from cannabis contains the same constituents (apart from nicotine) as tobacco smoke, including bronchial irritants, tumour initiators (mutagens), tumour promoters and carcinogens. The tar from cannabis smoke also contains greater concentrations of benzanthracenes and benzpyrenes, both of which are carcinogens, than the tar in tobacco smoke.

Pharmacokinetics

Cannabinoids remain in the body for a very long time; it takes up to one month to eliminate a single dose of THC obtained from one cannabis cigarette. Due to the fat-soluble nature of THC, 50% persists for

nearly one week, and 10% for one month in the brain. Therefore, the brain of a person who smokes cannabis only once weekly is never free of THC. This contrasts to alcohol, which is usually eliminated from the body within 24 hours.

Lung damage

In 2002, the British Lung Foundation published a report on *Cannabis – a smoking gun?* Summarising the published evidence, this report finds that 3-4 cannabis cigarettes a day are associated with the same evidence of acute and chronic bronchitis and the same degree of damage to the bronchial mucosa as 20 or more tobacco cigarettes a day.

Long-term effects of habitual cannabis smoking include a significantly higher prevalence of chronic and acute respiratory symptoms such as chronic cough, chronic sputum production, wheeze and acute bronchitis by comparison to non-smokers.

There have been several reports of severe lung damage including severe emphysema occurring in young people aged under 30, which is different in nature and clearly occurs at a younger age than the emphysema and bronchitis that cigarette smokers develop.

Cannabis, cancer and the immune system

While a causal relationship cannot be established, there are a number of case studies reporting cancers of the pharynx, larynx and mouth in young adults with a history of cannabis use. These cancers rarely occur under the age of 60.

Smoking cannabis is also associated with a weakened immune system in that it adversely affects the functioning of T cells, natural killer cells and macrophages that help protect the airways against micro-organisms. Macrophagal ability to produce a variety of chemicals that play a key role in the immune response to infection and malignancy has also shown to be impaired by cannabis smoking.

Effect on the developing baby of smoking cannabis during pregnancy

A study of 12,000 British women found that weekly use of cannabis during pregnancy may be associated with a small reduction in birth weight. An American study found that babies born to mothers who had used cannabis (as demonstrated by a positive urine test) had a small reduction in birth weight and length.

Cannabis and driving – if you've had a joint today, don't drive tomorrow!

Cannabis has been shown in many studies to affect motor control, impairing balance, tracking ability, hand-eye co-ordination, reaction time and physical strength. Even with a very low dose of 20mg of THC driving skills deteriorate. (A single joint can have up to 300mg of THC.) Due to its fat-soluble properties, cannabis persists in the body far longer than alcohol: airline pilots could not land their planes properly on flight simulators, even 24 hours after only 20mg of THC. Most pilots were unaware of a problem. In an Australian study of drivers under the age of 45 killed in traffic accidents over a four-year period, more than one-third of drivers were found to have evidence for recent cannabis use but either no alcohol or only very low blood alcohol levels.

The risk of developing cannabis dependence is probably of the same order as that of alcohol dependence, around 10-15%

The adverse effects of even a low dose of cannabis combined with alcohol were markedly greater than for either drug alone.

Effect on learning and educational performance

Heavy users of cannabis (those who smoked the drug at least 27 of the preceding 30 days) had significantly impaired skills related to attention, memory, and learning even after they had not used the drug for at least 24 hours. The heavy cannabis users had more trouble sustaining and shifting their attention and in registering, organising, and using information than did the study participants who had used cannabis no more than 3 of the previous 30 days. Students who smoke cannabis get lower grades and are less likely to graduate from high school, compared to their non-smoking peers. In another study, the verbal and mathematical skills of cannabis-smoking and non-smoking 12th-graders were compared. Although all of the students had scored equally well in 4th grade, the marijuana smokers' scores were significantly lower in 12th grade. While it may be impossible to entirely attribute the lower grades to cannabis use, the adverse effect on educational achievement warrants concern.

Cannabis addiction?

Cannabis has the potential for dependency and fulfils all the criteria for drug dependence, including a withdrawal syndrome, tolerance, escalation of dosage, craving, increasing importance of drug taking over other activities, and difficulty in controlling use. The risk of developing cannabis dependence is probably of the same order as that of alcohol dependence, around 10-15%.

Marijuana and madness

There is now considerable clinical evidence linking cannabis use to mental illness, especially schizophrenia, psychosis, anxiety and depression. The risk of developing mental illness, especially psychosis, is increased with earlier and heavier cannabis use. Over the past three decades, a doubling of the prevalence of schizophrenia has been observed in London. While it is too early to say whether this is due to the increase in cannabis abuse over the past decades, this possibility cannot be discounted on current evidence.

Patients with recent onset of psychosis are twice as likely to have used cannabis (but not alcohol or other illicit drugs) compared with a population without psychosis. Psychotic symptoms in conditions such as schizophrenia are mediated by dopamine, and THC raises the level of cerebral dopamine.

The first study linking cannabis use to mental illness was published in 1987. 50,000 Swedish conscripts were asked about their consumption of cannabis. Those who admitted at age 18 to having taken cannabis on more than 50 occasions, were nearly seven times more likely to develop schizophrenia in the following 15 years. These findings were largely ignored. However, over the past two years, several other studies confirm the link between cannabis and mental illness. A recent Dutch study of some 4,000 people in the general population showed that those taking large amounts of cannabis at the initial interview were almost seven times more likely to have psychotic symptoms three years later. Even a group of initially healthy individuals had an increased risk of psychosis. Cannabis use increases the risk of both the incidence of psychosis in psychosis-free persons and a poor prognosis for those with an established vulnerability to psychotic disorder. Critics argued that the findings of the Swedish and Dutch studies could have been caused by those individuals who were already developing schizophrenia, rather than by the use of cannabis. Two further studies have, however, excluded this hypothesis. An expansion of the Swedish Army study demonstrated that the results held even when initial personality was taken into account. The increased risk of schizophrenia with cannabis use was found to be the case even when people who may have been in the early stages of mental illness at the time of initial recruitment were excluded.

In a general population birth cohort study in Dunedin, New Zealand, it was found that those who used cannabis at age 15 were 4.5 times at higher risk of developing psychosis by age 26 than those starting cannabis at age 18. When the presence of psychotic-like ideas at the age of 11 was taken into account, the risk of schizophrenic symptoms at 26 was diminished, but was still important. Cannabis use in adolescence was a risk factor for experiencing symptoms

of schizophrenia in adulthood, over and above psychotic symptoms prior to cannabis use.

Reclassification of cannabis

Cannabis is certainly harmful and remains illegal after the downgrading of cannabis. It may be that the reclassification of cannabis will send out the message that cannabis is harmless and legal, thereby increasing cannabis abuse with all the adverse effects on an already overstretched NHS. It is vital that whatever view doctors may have about cannabis and its position in the classification league table that they are not blind to the potentially harmful effects that it may have on their patients.

■ The above article was written by Dr Hans-Christian Raabe, MD MRCP MRCGP DRCOG GP, The Family Practice, Leigh, Lancs.

© The Maranatha Community

Cannabis is blamed as cause of man's death

By Richard Savill

A man of 36 is believed to have become the first person in Britain to die directly from cannabis poisoning.

Lee Maisey smoked six cannabis cigarettes a day for 11 years, an inquest heard. His death, which was registered as having been caused by cannabis toxicity, led to new warnings about the drug, which was reclassified in January 2004 as a less dangerous one.

'This type of death is extremely rare,' Prof John Henry, a toxicologist at Imperial College, London, said after the inquest at Haverfordwest, west Wales.

'I have not seen anything like this before. It corrects the argument that cannabis cannot kill anybody.'

The inquest heard that Mr Maisey had complained of a headache on 22 August last year. Next morning he was found dead at the house he shared with a friend, Jeffrey Saunders, in Summerhill, Pembrokeshire.

Michael Howells, the Pembrokeshire coroner, said Mr Maisey was free from disease and had not drunk alcohol for at least 48 hours. Post-mortem tests showed a high level of cannabinoids in his blood.

He recorded a verdict of death by misadventure because Mr Maisey had died while taking part in an illegal activity. The death led to a warning about the changing strength of cannabis, which is to be reduced to a Class C drug on 29 January.

Dr Philip Guy, a lecturer in addictions at the University of Hull, said: 'Cannabis is not the nice hippy drug it used to be. It has been experimented with to produce stronger varieties.'

Dr Guy said that death was more likely if users ate the drug rather than smoked it. 'I would not be surprised if in this case the deceased had ingested a fatal amount of cannabis.'

Last autumn police issued a warning that big consignments of strong cannabis were being smuggled in from Africa.

The shadow home secretary, David Davis, said last night: 'This highlights what we have been saying about the effects of cannabis all along. When will people wake up to the fact that cannabis can be a harmful drug?

'By reclassifying the drug David Blunkett has shown he has lost the war on drugs. In my eyes, it's nothing more than an admission of failure.'

Tristan Millington-Drake, the chief executive of the Chemical Dependency Centre, a charity that provides treatment for people with drug problems, said: 'We have always taken the view that cannabis is an addictive drug, unlike the peddlers who try to persuade us that it is harmless. The Government's decision to reclassify cannabis is a mistake.'

© Telegraph Group Limited, London 2004

Drug-driving

How policymakers have overlooked potential indirect harm from cannabis use

The potential costs from people performing risky activities such as driving whilst under the influence of cannabis have been largely overlooked by those responsible for drugs policy, according to new research sponsored by the ESRC.

A study led by Dr Philip Terry, of the University of Birmingham, surveyed 100 frequent and 90 casual users of cannabis, and found that 52 per cent of the total (and 74 per cent of drivers) had driven a motor vehicle while under the influence of the substance. Of those who had, more than 70 per cent believed it had impaired their driving.

Dr Terry said: 'Previous studies have failed to examine the extent to which chronic use of cannabis is likely to increase someone's risk of accident or injury, or to have potentially significant adverse effects on their financial or social well-being by affecting their job performance or personal relationships.'

The study reveals that whilst 64 per cent of drivers among frequent users considered cannabis to impair their performance, 41 per cent felt it acceptable to drive whilst under the influence of the drug. This compares with 19 per cent of occasional users. One-third of frequent users were willing to drive even when 'very high' on cannabis.

Although 24 people had been stopped by the police while driving under the influence of the drug, none had been tested for cannabis intoxication or charged with driving while intoxicated.

The study reveals that whilst 64 per cent of drivers among frequent users considered cannabis to impair their performance, 41 per cent felt it acceptable to drive whilst under the influence of the drug

---

Nearly 80 per cent of those who had driven while or after using cannabis said they would be deterred from doing so if roadside testing were introduced.

For the study, those using the drug between two and seven days a week were regarded as frequent users, whilst infrequent users were those indulging, at most, four days per month.

The vast majority said they had used other legal and illegal drugs, often at the same time as cannabis. Ninety-seven per cent took alcohol, with 85 per cent doing so with cannabis, says the report. And 40 per cent used illegal drugs – mainly cocaine and ecstasy.

Sixty-five per cent of users showed some degree of dependence on cannabis, and more than 20 per cent reported that they experienced problems because of this. Many also had problems because of their involvement with other drugs.

Not surprisingly, perhaps, frequent users showed more signs of dependence, with more than a third speaking of concerns over problems associated specifically with cannabis.

Compared with infrequent users, they reported considerably more guilt and greater incidence of medical problems related to their cannabis use, as well as more neglect of their families. Yet the

study found that only two per cent of the total 190 users surveyed had received counselling or treatment for cannabis abuse.

Significant numbers claimed positive effects of using cannabis, including aiding sleep (77 per cent), pain relief (50 per cent) and heightened sexual pleasure (79 per cent). Eighty-five per cent cited relaxation as a benefit, and 75 per cent sharing and socialising with others.

However, significant numbers also spoke of negative effects of cannabis use. During interviews, effects most frequently reported were paranoia (55 per cent), demotivation (53 per cent) and memory impairment (47 per cent).

A quarter of those in the study said they used cannabis before or at work, and just over half of these admitted to some degree of impair-

---

Significant numbers also spoke of negative effects of cannabis use. During interviews, effects most frequently reported were paranoia, demotivation and memory impairment

---

ment. However, use did not seem to result in more absenteeism, workplace accidents or injuries, or frequent job changes.

■ The research report *Indirect Harm From Regular Cannabis Use* was funded by the Economic and Social Research Council (ESRC). The author, Dr Philip Terry, is at the

School of Psychology, University of Birmingham, Birmingham, B15 2TT.

The ESRC is the UK's largest funding agency for research and postgraduate training relating to social and economic issues. It provides independent, high-quality, relevant research to business, the public sector and Government. The ESRC invests more than £76 million every year in social science and at any time is supporting some 2,000 researchers in academic institutions and research policy institutes. It also funds postgraduate training within the social sciences to nurture the researchers of tomorrow. More at www.esrc.ac.uk Copies of the report are available from comms@esrc.ac.uk

Source: Economic and Social Research Council (ESRC)

© Dr Philip Terry

Medical use of cannabis approved

By Andrew Osborn

The Netherlands yesterday (1 September 2003) became the first country to legalise the medical use of cannabis, allowing doctors to prescribe the narcotic as a painkiller for those who are seriously ill.

In a move that is certain to put pressure on other countries to follow suit, chemists began selling the drug for a price of between €40 and €50 (£27 to £33) for a 5g (0.18oz) bag.

Although that is approximately twice the cost of buying the drug in one of the country's 1,500 coffee shops, the government claimed that there was a huge difference in quality.

It also said that the costs incurred by patients may be re-imbursed by public health insurers.

Medicinal cannabis – which will be sold in the form of dried marijuana flowers from the hemp plant – is being grown to order by two official suppliers, it added, and rigorously tested for impurities.

It will be prescribed as a painkiller for people suffering from

cancer, Aids, multiple sclerosis or Tourette's syndrome, but only if more conventional drugs have failed or caused unwanted side effects.

Medicinal cannabis – which will be sold in the form of dried marijuana flowers from the hemp plant – is being grown to order by two official suppliers and rigorously tested for impurities

---

The health ministry estimates that up to 7,000 people in the Netherlands already regularly use cannabis for medical reasons and

believes that the number could double once the new scheme takes off.

'Cannabis has a beneficial effect for many patients,' it said in a statement.

Analysts said that Britain and parts of the United States, Australia and Canada were all considering following suit, and they would be carefully monitoring the Dutch experience.

The Dutch government is keen, however, to dispel the image of spliff-wielding patients.

It is recommending that the drug be diluted and used to make marijuana tea or administered in a special spray mechanism.

Nor is the move without controversy.

Although the drug is widely credited as an effective painkiller, some doctors argue that it increases the risk of depression and schizophrenia.

© Guardian Newspapers Limited 2003

The legal position on cannabis

Information from RELEASE

What is the legal position?

It is illegal to possess, supply, cultivate, produce, import or export cannabis.

Cannabis (including cannabinol, cannabinol derivatives and cannabis oil) has been reclassified as a Class C drug.

Simple possession

Simple possession now carries a maximum two-year custodial sentence or a fine. The police still have the power to arrest for possession of cannabis, although this is not the case in relation to other Class C drugs.

However, the Association of Chief Police Officers (ACPO) have issued guidance to the police force that there should be a presumption against arrest where someone is in possession of a small amount of cannabis (that is, where it is clearly for personal use).

In such cases, unless there are aggravating factors, a warning will be given and the cannabis will be confiscated. According to the ACPO guidelines, aggravating factors include smoking in public, being repeatedly caught in possession of cannabis, and having cannabis in your possession while in the vicinity of children. There are other factors, and you should contact our legal helpline or consult your solicitor for further information.

It is important to remember that the presumption against arrest is at the discretion of the police officer involved. It is not a legal right.

Supply offences

The penalty for supply offences has increased from 5 years' to 14 years' imprisonment.

Young people

The law has not changed in relation to young people and cannabis. Young people caught in possession of cannabis WILL STILL be arrested under the Crime and Disorder Act [1998] which requires young offenders to be dealt with at the police station. The presumption against arrest DOES NOT apply to young people.

Occupiers of premises

It remains illegal for occupiers of premises, or anyone concerned in the management of premises, to allow those premises to be used for the production, supply or smoking of cannabis.

This law has been amended to cover the use or administering of any controlled drug. However, the amendment has not yet come into force. For further information as to the current position, please call our legal helpline or consult your solicitor.

Sentencing

Sentences for possession are usually limited to fines and only in exceptional circumstances will a tougher sentence be imposed. Many first-time offenders will simply receive a caution. However, the sentences for supply or intent to supply can be harsher. Sentences for any drug offence depend upon the quantities involved, previous convictions and other relevant circumstances.

Driving

Being unfit to drive under the influence of any intoxicant, including cannabis, is an offence which is likely to lead to the loss of your driving licence. Getting your licence back and obtaining insurance after losing it are likely to be difficult.

Further information

For further information please call our legal helpline on 020 7749 9904 or consult your solicitor.

© RELEASE

Cannabis reclassification

Frequently asked questions, answered by the Home Office

Why has the Government reclassified cannabis?

The Advisory Council on the Misuse of Drugs advised that cannabis is harmful, but not as harmful as other Class B drugs, such as the amphetamines.

Reclassification brings the law into line with this assessment, and will enable the Government to give a more credible message to young people about the relative dangers of drugs.

The change will enable the Government to focus more effectively on Class A drugs – hard drugs such as heroin and crack/cocaine which cause the most harm – and on getting people into treatment.

What is the legal effect of reclassification?

Cannabis, as a Class C drug, remains controlled under the Misuse of Drugs Act; and possessing it remains a criminal offence, but the maximum penalties for possession are reduced from 5 years' to 2 years' imprisonment. Maximum penalties for supplying and dealing in cannabis stay at 14 years' imprisonment.

What laws have changed in connection with the reclassification of cannabis?

There are 2 changes:

- Retaining the power of arrest for cannabis possession offences (under guidance being issued by the police, there is a presumption against this power being used, unless there are specific aggravating factors).
- Increasing the maximum penalty for supply and dealing in Class C drugs from 5 years' to 14 years' imprisonment. This means that, on reclassification, the maximum penalty for trafficking cannabis remains 14 years' imprisonment, and the courts continue to be able to impose substantial sentences for serious dealing offences.

Why are drugs classified A, B or C?

The Misuse of Drugs Act 1971 places drugs into one of three categories, A, B or C, for the purposes of control. Classification broadly reflects the risks and harms caused by misuse of the controlled drug in question, and is reflected in penalty levels for drugs offences.

What is the Advisory Council on the Misuse of Drugs?

This is the statutory, independent Government advisory body tasked to keep drug misuse and the legislation under review, and to advise the Government on the need for any changes.

The membership of this group comprises experience and expertise in a range of disciplines related to drug misuse.

How is a drug reclassified?

An Order in Council is needed to move cannabis from the list of Class B drugs to Class C. The Order in Council is debated in, and has to be approved by, the Commons and Lords and has to be approved by the Privy Council.

What do UN Conventions require?

The United Kingdom is signatory to three UN conventions on international co-operation in the drugs field. These require contracting states to establish as criminal offences the possession, production or cultivation of many drugs, including cannabis, for personal consumption.

What was the date of reclassification?

29 January 2004.

What will happen to someone who is found in possession of cannabis?

Under the guidance being issued by the Association of Chief Police Officers (ACPO) to all police forces, there will be a presumption against arrest. For adults, most offences of cannabis possession are likely to result in a warning and confiscation of the drug. But the following instances may lead to arrest and possible caution or prosecution:

- repeat offending
- smoking in a public place
- instances where public order is threatened
- possession of cannabis in the vicinity of premises used by children

This is operational from the date of reclassification, 29 January 2004.

By retaining the power of arrest, aren't you just maintaining the status quo? What will change?

There will be a presumption against arrest under the police guidance – at present there is no such presumption. In addition, following reclassification, the maximum penalty for the

Will the reclassification of cannabis encourage greater use?

There is no reason why it should. It remains an illegal drug and criminal sanctions continue to apply. In particular, the Government intends to take a tough line with dealers. It is backing up reclassification with an education campaign aimed at young people, to make it clear how the law will operate in practice and to dissuade them from experimenting with cannabis.

The Advisory Council report on cannabis indicates that: 'In attempting to analyse the likely impact on prevalence of reclassification, there is very little relevant domestic learning to draw on. But it is possible to look at the experience of other countries, albeit in circumstances where civil penalties have replaced criminal sanctions. In particular, the experiences in Australia, the Netherlands and the United States are illustrative. In each of these countries a reduction in the penalties for using cannabis has not led to a significant increase in use.'

possession of cannabis will go down from 5 years' to 2 years' imprisonment.

Reclassification sends a more credible message to young people that all drugs are harmful, but some are more harmful than others.

Why are young people being dealt with more strictly than adults?

They are not being dealt with more strictly – they are likely to receive reprimands or warnings for a first offence of cannabis possession. However, the process is more formal for persons under 18, and it is important that their cases should be dealt with at the police station, so that any underlying problems with the young person can be identified.

Young people under the age of 18 who receive a final warning, or are reported for court proceedings for the possession of cannabis, will be referred to the local Youth Offending Team (YOT), and are likely to have their substance misuse assessed by the YOT drugs worker, who may arrange treatment or other support where this is needed.

Does reclassification mean people are able to smoke openly?

No. Those who smoke openly in public face possible arrest and prosecution.

How can you ensure that the police enforce the law in a consistent way and don't overuse the power of arrest?

The Association of Chief Police Officers (ACPO) is committed to the guidance, and to ensuring that it is

How will young people under 18 be dealt with?

The Government is sending out a clear message to young people under 18 that cannabis misuse remains illegal.

Police enforcement will be consistent with the more structured framework for early juvenile offending established under the Crime and Disorder Act 1998, where a young offender can receive a reprimand, final warning or charge depending on the seriousness of the offence. Following one reprimand, any further offence will lead to a final warning or charge.

Any further offence following a warning will normally result in a charge being brought. After a final warning, the young offender must be referred to the Youth Offending Team to arrange a rehabilitation programme to prevent reoffending.

operated consistently and within its spirit.

ACPO will keep its operation under constant review, particularly in its early stages. In addition, HM Chief Inspector of Constabulary will closely monitor the guidance's use, and will intervene with any police force where necessary.

On reclassification, the maximum penalty for trafficking cannabis remains 14 years' imprisonment

---

What action are you taking against those people who intend to set up cannabis cafés?

Anyone trying to establish a cannabis café risks imprisonment or a heavy fine (or both). Supply of cannabis remains a criminal offence, and those who sell it to others risk severe penalties. It is also an offence for managers of premises to allow smoking or supply of cannabis on their premises.

Reclassification of cannabis makes no difference to this position. We expect the police to respond swiftly and effectively to any such attempts to defy the law. Smoking cannabis in a cannabis café (or elsewhere) could result in arrest and prosecution.

Why are we not adopting the Dutch model?

In Holland, the small-scale possession and supply of cannabis remain illegal but there is a formal policy of tolerance of small-scale selling and possession of cannabis in coffee shops. But coffee shops still have to go to the criminal markets for their supplies.

Dutch experience also shows us how difficult it is to restrict the sale of cannabis, including to children, through a licensed source.

Why is the Government not moving towards a controlled regime for cannabis?

The report does not make a direct comparison between cannabis and alcohol and tobacco. The introduction of a controlled regime for cannabis similar to the licensed

regimes attached to the sale of alcohol and tobacco would lead, among other things, to a significant increase in consumption – a simple comparison with the number of alcohol and tobacco users is illustrative.

Increased use would significantly add to public health costs and could encourage wider consumption of drugs and further drug addiction. A regulated supply would also increase the availability of drugs to children.

What are the harmful effects of cannabis?

The acute effects include damage to people's ability to learn and carry out many tasks, including operating machinery and driving vehicles. Acute cannabis intoxication can also lead to panic attacks, paranoia and confused feelings.

The chronic effects include damage to mental functioning and in particular to learning difficulties, which in prolonged and heavy users may not necessarily be reversible. A cannabis dependence syndrome has been identified in heavy users and the drug can exacerbate schizophrenia in people who are already affected. Smoking cannabis over a long period of time can lead to respiratory diseases, including lung cancer.

What about reports that cannabis use leads to mental illness?

Some research suggests that heavy cannabis use over a long period might lead to schizophrenia, but other research suggests it does not. The overall evidence is inconclusive. What is clear is that cannabis use can worsen schizophrenia which already exists.

What about reports that cannabis smoking leads to lung cancer?

Smoking cannabis presents a real health risk, potentially similar to that of tobacco. Smoked cannabis has a higher concentration of certain carcinogens than smoked tobacco, and it tends to be inhaled more deeply.

However, in general cannabis smokers smoke fewer cigarettes per day than tobacco smokers and most give up in their 30s. A Department

of Health working group is examining the health consequences of cannabis smoking.

Is cannabis a 'gateway' drug leading to use of more harmful drugs? Won't this lead to more people taking hard drugs?

The evidence for cannabis as a 'gateway' drug, which leads on to other drug use, is inconclusive. Research confirms that establishing a causal link is extremely difficult. It is clear that most users of the more dangerous drugs used cannabis earlier in their careers, but most cannabis users do not go on to use other drugs regularly.

Of course, the same can be said of alcohol. Very large numbers of those who use Class A drugs have used alcohol to excess. But many people who use alcohol do not progress to any form of other drug.

What are you doing to educate young people about the dangers of cannabis?

To coincide with reclassification, the

Some research suggests that heavy cannabis use over a long period might lead to schizophrenia, but other research suggests it does not

---

Government has issued a fact sheet which is widely available to young people, which explains that cannabis remains illegal and describes what will happen to someone who is found in possession of cannabis. The 3-year national campaign – FRANK – to alert young people to the harm of all drugs includes information about cannabis.

Will the Government permit the use of cannabis for medicinal purposes?

The Home Secretary has made it clear that he is willing to amend the misuse of drugs legislation as necessary, to allow the prescribing of a cannabis-based medicine as a form of pain relief. The Home Office granted a licence to GW Pharmaceuticals who have conducted trials and have developed a cannabis-based medicine designed to relieve chronic nerve pain.

The company are currently seeking marketing approval for the product from the Medicines and Healthcare Products Regulatory Agency – a process all new medicines have to go through which is designed to protect public health. The Multiple Sclerosis Society supports this approach.

■ The above information is from the Government's Tackling Drugs web site which can be found at www.drugs.gov.uk

© Crown copyright

Cannabis and the law

One in four believe sale of cannabis should be legalised

By Anthony King

The Home Secretary's decision to downgrade cannabis from a class B to a class C drug has majority support among the public, according to YouGov's survey for *The Daily Telegraph*.

The survey reveals that more than half of all adults would be happy to see its sale and possession decriminalised or even legalised.

The great majority reserve their fear and detestation for hard drugs such as heroin and crack cocaine. Nearly everyone believes these to be seriously addictive and almost invariably harmful to users.

The survey also reveals a gap amounting to a chasm between those under the age of 35 and older generations. Those born in the Seventies and Eighties share their elders' abhorrence of hard drugs but are much less convinced that the country suffers from a serious drugs problem or that soft drugs are a scourge.

The gap even extends to beliefs about which 'drugs' are addictive. The young, by a wide margin, reckon that tobacco, alcohol and coffee are all more addictive than cannabis and ecstasy. The old agree about the first two but are not so sure about coffee.

YouGov's survey is one of the most comprehensive to be conducted into the public's beliefs about drugs.

The pollsters began by asking people to assess the extent of the drugs problem in Britain. Roughly half of YouGov's respondents, 51 per cent, believe 'there is a serious drugs problem in this country and it affects practically the whole country'.

Somewhat fewer, 42 per cent, agree there is a serious problem but believe 'it is largely confined to certain neighbourhoods and certain kinds of people'. Already, however, the generation gap emerges. The under-35s are far more likely than their elders to reckon that there is no nationwide problem.

The young also differ sharply from the middle-aged and older people in wanting to distinguish clearly between hard and soft drugs. Opinion among the over-35s is almost evenly divided on the issue. Among the younger generation a substantial majority, 73 per cent, believe 'a distinction should be made between "hard" drugs such as heroin and crack cocaine and "soft" drugs such as cannabis'.

Asked which drugs are seriously addictive, people agree on putting heroin, crack cocaine, tobacco and alcohol at the top of the list and cannabis and ecstasy towards the bottom, though, once again, older generations are more suspicious than the young of so-called softer drugs.

On the connection between cannabis use and the abuse of hard drugs, the old and young are more closely aligned. Both groups broadly agree that cannabis users are more likely than others to use hard drugs but whereas only half of the 18-34 age group, exactly 50 per cent, believe cannabis users are 'a lot' or 'somewhat' more likely than others to resort to hard drugs, that proportion among older people rises to nearly two-thirds, 63 per cent.

In other words, younger people are considerably more likely than their elders to see drug abuse as varied and complex rather than uniform.

Asked what they believe establishes any connection that exists between hard- and soft-drug use, an

Drugs and the law

With regard to soft drugs such as cannabis, which statement comes closest to your own view?

	All	18-34s	Over-35s
The sale and possession of soft drugs should remain a criminal offence, as now	43	33	48
Selling or possessing them should remain illegal but should be regarded as a minor offence, such as parking in the wrong place, rather than a criminal offence	28	33	27
Selling or possessing them should no longer be illegal	23	31	19
Don't know	6	4	7

With regard to hard drugs such as heroin and crack cocaine, which statement comes closest to your own view?

	All	18-34s	Over-35s
The sale and possession of hard drugs should remain a criminal offence, as now	89	87	90
Selling or possessing them should remain illegal but should be regarded as a minor offence, such as parking in the wrong place, rather than a criminal offence	4	5	3
Selling or possessing them should no longer be illegal	5	6	5
Don't know	2	2	2

From 29 January 2004, cannabis was downgraded from class B to a class C drug, meaning in practice that, although selling and possessing it is still illegal, people who use it in private are unlikely to be prosecuted. Do you approve or disapprove of this change in the law?

	All	18-34s	Over-35s
Approve	52	63	46
Disapprove	39	28	44
Don't know	10	9	10

Source: Telegraph YouGov Poll, January 2004

overwhelming majority of YouGov's respondents, 83 per cent, appear to be clear that the problem arises not from cannabis creating a craving for harder drugs but 'because some people who use cannabis find themselves part of a "drug culture" with dealers pushing both hard and soft drugs'.

The belief that pushers have a financial interest in selling both soft and hard drugs – and in encouraging soft-drug users to move on to the hard stuff – may help explain the widespread support for cannabis being decriminalised and even legalised. Almost everyone believes that hard drugs harm all or most of those who use them.

However, there is nothing approaching unanimity on the issue of whether soft drugs such as cannabis also cause harm. Among the young, 53 per cent reckon cannabis harms either none of those who use it or only a minority but among the over-35s, almost exactly the same proportion, 50 per cent, reckon that cannabis, on the contrary, harms all or most of those who use it.

No one disputes that the sale and use of drugs leads to the commission of additional drug-related crimes. The main issue in dispute is the link between the two. The great majority of YouGov's respondents are in no doubt. Fully 91 per cent believe drug addicts turn to crime 'because they steal to get money to buy drugs'. Only a small minority, seven per cent, attribute drug-related crime primarily to 'mental instability'. The section of the survey headed 'Drugs and the law' presents probably YouGov's most striking findings: only a minority of people, 43 per cent, believe that 'the sale and possession of soft drugs such as cannabis should remain a criminal offence'.

A clear majority, 51 per cent, including no fewer than 64 per cent among the under-35s, believe that cannabis should either become a minor offence ('decriminalised') or even no offence at all ('legalised'). Almost exactly the same proportion, 52 per cent, applaud David Blunkett's decision to reclassify cannabis as a relatively harmless class C drug. That said, the present very hard line on

Younger people are considerably more likely than their elders to see drug abuse as varied and complex rather than uniform

hard drugs remains. Fewer than 10 per cent of YouGov's respondents favour changing the law in any respect.

If the laws on drugs were changed, a large proportion – 56 per cent among the young rising to 67 per cent among older generations – reckon that drug use would increase. The fact that many of these same people favour relaxing the existing laws on cannabis probably means that they think the increase would be mainly among cannabis rather than hard-drug users.

YouGov elicited the opinions of 2,536 adults across Britain online between 20 and 22 Jan. The data have been weighted to conform to the demographic profile of British adults as a whole.

■ Anthony King is professor of government at Essex University.
© *Telegraph Group Limited, London 2004*

Simple and powerful rebuttals of common arguments

Many false arguments are being circulated to justify reclassification. Here are some of those arguments, each with a simple rebuttal.

Reclassification puts out a more effective message about the harm caused by cannabis.
The current law is clear. Cocaine is a class A drug, cannabis is a class B drug. Cannabis is far too dangerous to be shunted into class C – to be put on the same level as sleeping pills.

Cannabis is not a very harmful drug.
Cannabis is a very harmful mind-altering drug. It is responsible for a rising proportion of road deaths, it causes schizophrenia and cancer.

We need to focus on class A drugs to save police time.
The police concentrate on class A drugs already. As the 'gateway' evidence shows, if more people take cannabis, more people will go on to take harder drugs. This approach is totally self-defeating.

The Advisory Council on the Misuse of Drugs recommended reclassification.
The ACMD report also warned 'Since cannabis use has only become commonplace in the past 30 years there may be worse news to come.'[1]

Cannabis use is so common that the current law is unworkable.
According to the *British Crime Survey*, 66% of people aged 16-59 in England and Wales have never used an illegal drug.[2] Also, the fact that a large number of people break a law is not a good reason for scrapping it. The Government is not proposing to abolish speed limits.

References
1 *The Classification of Drugs under the Misuse of Drugs Act 1971*, ACMD, Home Office, 2002, page 7
2 Aust, R, Sharp, C and Goulden, C, *Prevalence of Drug Use: Key Findings from the 2001/2002 British Crime Survey*, Findings 182, Home Office, 2002, page 2

© *The Christian Institute, October 2003*

Government ads aim to end confusion

One simple message: law is being relaxed but drug is still harmful and remains illegal

By Alan Travis, Home Affairs Editor

A big government advertising campaign to dispel the confusion surrounding the change in cannabis laws and targeted to reach more than 80% of Britain's teenagers was launched by the Home Office yesterday.

Radio advertisements will be carried on 48 national and regional stations in England promoting the 'one simple message' that although the cannabis laws are being relaxed next week (29 January 2004) it is still a harmful drug that remains illegal.

Separate campaigns will run in Scotland, Wales and Northern Ireland. The campaigns will be backed up by the distribution of more than 2.5 million leaflets explaining the impact of moving cannabis from class B to class C in the schedule of illegal drugs.

The initiative will be accompanied by a police campaign to promote a similar message to adults and an internal police campaign to ensure that all officers are aware of the changes in the law.

Police advertisements setting out the change in the law as it affects adults are to appear in the *Sun*, *Daily Mirror*, *Daily Telegraph*, *Guardian* and *News of the World*.

The Home Office drugs minister, Caroline Flint, said that the radio ads and the leaflets had been months in the making. 'They have been fully researched and tested with young people to make sure the message is both effective and credible to our target audience,' she said. 'It is particularly important that we get the message across to young people that cannabis remains illegal and that under-18s will still be arrested for possession.

'Using the radio ads alone we expect to reach 81% of 15- to 17-year-olds and 41% of adults.'

The home secretary, David Blunkett, defended the decision to reclassify cannabis, saying there was little point in pretending to young people that it was as dangerous as crack cocaine and heroin.

The change, which comes into effect 29 January 2004, was first recommended by the government's advisory committee on drug abuse more than 20 years ago.

> **Advertisements will promote the 'one simple message' that although the cannabis laws are being relaxed next week it is still a harmful drug that remains illegal**

Mr Blunkett dismissed criticism earlier this week from the British Medical Association which said that chronic cannabis smoking can increase the likelihood of heart disease, lung cancer, bronchitis and emphysema.

The home secretary claimed this was a reversal of the BMA welcome that greeted his announcement two years ago that the law would be relaxed.

He insisted that the government was not sending out a confused message.

He said: 'I want a transparent, non-variable, understandable policy across the country, where we as politicians take hands-on responsibility for the decisions about classification, and therefore the response, whether the police go for class A dangerous drug pushers and users that kill or whether we go for small possession of cannabis.'

Currently, individual forces adopt their own policies towards cannabis possession.

'It is also important that we respond to the cry from some families of drug users who said to me that if you confuse our children by saying pretty much that cannabis is the same

as crack or heroin, when they take cannabis and find out it isn't, they don't believe the message when they go on to heroin and crack,' Mr Blunkett said.

Further mixed signals from Downing Street on drugs policy include the latest 'blue skies' thinking from Lord Birt, who has reportedly suggested prison sentences of up to seven years for heroin use. Such a move would meet resistance, not least because the further criminalisation of addicts contradicts current thinking on treatment rather than prison.

Meanwhile the British Lung Foundation said it welcomed the government's advertising campaign on reclassification, but reminded people of the health risks involved.

Its chief executive, Dame Helena Shovelton, said: 'Research carried out by the charity found that smoking cannabis alone can cause severe lung damage.

'We understand that some people with long-term chronic conditions may smoke cannabis for medicinal purposes, but it is vital that people are fully aware of the dangers.'

Learning a lesson

- From 29 January 2004 cannabis will be reclassified as a class C drug, which covers the least harmful of the illegal drugs, including GHB, anabolic steroids and tranquillisers such as Valium.
- It will remain illegal to have, give away or deal in cannabis. Possession with intent to supply is also illegal, as is growing cannabis plants. Dealing and possessing with intent to supply will still carry a 14-year maximum sentence plus an unlimited fine.
- The penalties for possession are changing. The maximum prison sentence is being reduced from five years to two. New police guidelines will mean that what happens to most of the 90,000 people a year who are currently arrested for cannabis possession will change.
- If you are over 18 and the police find you with cannabis it is likely that it will be confiscated and

you will be warned. But if you are smoking a joint in a public place, or near where there are children, such as a school, or where public order is at risk, you will be arrested and possibly fined. Those re-

peatedly arrested for cannabis offences will be prosecuted.
- If you are under 18 and it is your first offence of cannabis possession you will normally be arrested, taken to a police station and given a warning or reprimand. But if you have been caught before, you will either be given a final warning or be charged. When you get a warning you are referred to the local youth offending team.
- It remains illegal to pass drugs among friends or allow people to smoke cannabis in your home; and if you are caught smoking cannabis in a club the police will have the power to prosecute the landlord or the club owner.

© Guardian Newspapers Limited 2004

ACPO publish cannabis enforcement guidelines

Chief police officers have issued new guidelines on policing cannabis possession following the Government's proposal to reclassify cannabis from a Class B to a Class C drug.

Announcing the new policing enforcement guidelines, Andy Hayman, Chairman of the ACPO Drugs Sub-Committee and Chief Constable of Norfolk Constabulary, said:

'Following a period of consultation these guidelines have been developed to provide police officers with straightforward operational guidance for dealing with simple cases of possession by adult offenders.

'The proposed reclassification of cannabis will mean that officers will still have a power of arrest for simple possession. In the spirit of the Home Secretary's decision to reclassify cannabis, the new guidance recommends that there should be a presumption against arrest. In practice, this means that in the majority of cases officers will issue a warning and confiscate the drug. Police officers will be expected to use their discretion and take the circumstances of each case into account before deciding whether to arrest or not.

'The guidance suggests that arrest will be considered in circumstances such as the smoking of cannabis in public view, repeated possession of the drug, public disorder as a result of cannabis possession or possessing cannabis in the vicinity of premises frequented by young people, such as schools and youth clubs. Young people (under-18s) who are found in possession of cannabis will receive a formal warning at a police station.

'The reclassification of cannabis will allow police to focus more time and resources on Class A drugs. That said, despite reclassification, it remains illegal to possess cannabis.'

The cannabis enforcement guidance became operational in early 2004.

- The above information is from ACPO's web site which can be found at www.acpo.police.uk

© ACPO

Policing cannabis

Police will let most cannabis users off with verbal warning

By John Steele, Crime Correspondent

Police should no longer arrest the majority of people found in possession of small amounts of cannabis for personal use, according to new guidelines issued on 11 September 2003 by the Association of Chief Police Officers.

Instead, offenders should receive a verbal warning on the street after giving their details and admitting possession of the drug, which would then be confiscated. Such a warning will not constitute a criminal record.

However, the power of arrest for cannabis possession will remain. Officers can use their discretion to arrest if: the drug is consumed in public; the person is a repeat user; the possession is deemed to create public order difficulties, or cause a 'locally identified policing problem'; or it is found around young people in places such as schools or youth clubs.

Those arrested may still face prosecution or conviction, or a formal caution, both of which leave a criminal record.

People under 18 found in possession of cannabis will receive a formal warning at a police station. Under-tens caught with the drug will be considered 'at risk'.

The Government has decided to reclassify cannabis from a Class B drug to a Class C substance to reduce the police time spent on arresting or formally cautioning people found in possession. The aim is to focus on Class A hard drugs such as heroin and cocaine.

David Blunkett, the Home Secretary, stressed that cannabis 'will not be legalised or decriminalised'.

Under existing law, police can arrest for Class B drug possession, but not for possession of Class C substances.

However, police did not want to lose the power of arrest in relation to cannabis. Therefore, as well as ordering the downgrading of cannabis, the Home Office has introduced a measure into the Criminal Justice Bill to retain the power of arrest. Both measures are scheduled to come into law in January 2004, when ACPO will activate its guidelines.

Andy Hayman, the chairman of the ACPO drugs sub-committee and Chief Constable of Norfolk, said: 'In the spirit of the Home Secretary's decision to reclassify cannabis, the

> ## 'In practice, this means that in the majority of cases officers will issue a warning and confiscate the drug'

new guidance recommends that there should be a presumption against arrest.

'In practice, this means that in the majority of cases officers will issue a warning and confiscate the drug. Police officers will be expected to use their discretion.

'The reclassification of cannabis will allow police to focus more time and resources on Class A drugs. That said, despite reclassification, it remains illegal to possess cannabis.'

The guidelines do not specify the quantity of cannabis defined as for simple personal possession, as this could encourage dealers to carry around only amounts smaller than the prescribed limit. Police would also face difficulties in judging amounts.

ACPO advises that street interviews 'should be short but sufficient to prove the offence or identify a defence. This could be as little as two questions, such as "What is this?" and "Whose is it?" This should be recorded contemporaneously in an officer's pocketbook.

'This would reduce paperwork and bureaucracy for patrol officers.'

Incidents of possession dealt with by warnings will still be recorded as 'cleared up' crimes.

© Telegraph Group Limited, London 2004

Seizures[1] of selected drugs

United Kingdom						Numbers
	1991	1995	1998	1999	2000	2001
Cannabis	59,420	90,935	114,691	98,450	91,695	93,482
Heroin	2,640	6,479	15,192	15,519	16,457	18,168
Ecstasy-type	1,735	5,521	4,850	6,637	9,784	10,411
Cocaine	1,446	2,270	5,209	5,858	6,005	6,984
Amphetamines	6,821	15,462	18,630	13,393	7,073	6,799
Crack	583	1,445	2,488	2,507	2,765	3,688
Methadone	427	942	1,584	1,215	1,171	1,072
LSD	1,636	1,158	623	480	297	168
All seizures	69,807	114,339	151,749	134,101	125,079	130,894

1 Seizures by the Police and HM Customs. A seizure can include more than one type of drug.

Source: 2001/02 British Crime Survey, Home Office, Crown copyright

Home cultivation of cannabis

Government urged to re-think penalties as more cannabis users 'grow their own'

Home cultivation of cannabis is so widespread that it may now account for as much as half of all consumption in Britain. But there are wide discrepancies in the way that police and the courts apply the laws against cultivation, which will be left unchanged after Government plans make possession of cannabis a less serious offence.

New research for the Joseph Rowntree Foundation highlights an increasing tendency for cannabis users to 'grow their own', making them less dependent on the international trade in narcotics. It suggests that some cultivation is by commercial dealers, but much is on a small scale for personal use or use by friends.

It also describes how the home-grown market is supported by a thriving, legal trade in cannabis seeds and horticultural equipment – including soil-less 'hydroponic' cultivation systems and lighting – that can be purchased through magazines, the internet and even garden centres.

The report is being published in the same week as the United Nations General Assembly Special Session (UNGASS) meets in Vienna to review international action against illegal drugs.

The researchers, at South Bank University's Criminal Policy Research Unit and the National Addiction Centre at King's College London, surveyed practice in English and Welsh police forces, reviewed the law and enforcement arrangements in other countries, and examined the requirements of the United Nations conventions on illicit drugs. They also surveyed 37 cannabis growers. Their findings led them to divide cannabis cultivators into five different groups:

- Sole-use growers, who cultivated cannabis for personal use or use with friends. They tended to view

cultivation as a hobby where they could save money and avoid contact with dealers.
- Medical growers, who used the drug to relieve the symptoms of long-term conditions, such as multiple sclerosis.
- Social growers, who wanted to ensure a good quality supply for themselves and friends.

The home-grown market is supported by a thriving, legal trade in cannabis seeds and horticultural equipment

---

- Social/commercial growers cultivating for themselves and friends, but also selling the cannabis to provide an income.
- Commercial growers cultivating the drug to make money and sell to any potential customer.

The cultivators who were interviewed used a variety of growing techniques, depending largely on their knowledge and technical expertise, and achieved very variable yields from their 'crops'.

Home Office statistics show that 458 offenders were cautioned for cannabis cultivation in 2000, while another 1,502 were convicted in court, including 243 who were sent to prison. However, the police survey revealed how similar offences were treated differently by different forces. Some forces charged growers with 'production', which carries a mandatory seven-year prison sentence for a third conviction, while others used the lesser offence of 'cultivation'.

David Blunkett, the Home Secretary, has announced that possession offences will usually attract on-the-spot warnings and confiscation when cannabis is reclassified as a Class C drug in January 2004. The report discusses ways in which the police and courts might treat cultivation of cannabis for personal use on a par with possession.

One possibility would be to leave the law unchanged, but for the police, prosecutors and the courts to receive guidance about the circumstances when home growers should be given on-the-spot warnings. This guidance could be based on the weight of cannabis or the number of confiscated plants.

Another option would be to create new offences of 'social supply' and 'social cultivation' of cannabis – defined as growing and distributing the drug non-commercially to friends – and for guidance to be issued about the way that these offences should be dealt with by the police and the courts.

The report notes that a UK decision to change the law so small-scale cultivation of cannabis was treated in a similar way to possession would not contravene the UN drug conventions. But it would bring British law into line with many other developed nations – including the Netherlands and Switzerland, where enforcement policy deliberately seeks to draw cannabis users away from criminal suppliers who may also try to sell them more harmful drugs like heroin and cocaine.

Prof. Mike Hough of South Bank University, co-author of the report, said: 'The Government has decided to reclassify cannabis as a Class C drug, with less serious penalties for possession. Yet debate has so far ignored the issue of cultivation and the opportunities for careful reform that would reduce the harm caused by dangerous drugs and drug dealing.

'Large minorities of young people use cannabis. It is essential to insulate them as much as possible from drug markets operated by dealers who sell not only cannabis but crack and heroin. If small-scale home cultivation attracted an on-the-spot warning rather than a caution or a court conviction, it is likely that more users would switch to growing their own and stop buying from dealers. As their profits from cannabis sales diminished, criminal entrepreneurs could be forced to abandon the cannabis market altogether.'

Dame Ruth Runciman, Chair of the Foundation's Drug and Alcohol Research Committee, and formerly Chair of the Police Foundation's Independent Inquiry into the Misuse of Drugs Act, said: 'I very much hope that the Government will pay close attention to the anomalies highlighted by this report and to the range of policy options that it identifies. In particular, it seems likely that a more careful

---

Home Office statistics show that 458 offenders were cautioned for cannabis cultivation in 2000

---

distinction in law between social and commercial cultivation could be used to drive a wedge between users and the criminally sophisticated gangs who might otherwise try to sell them more harmful, Class A drugs as well as cannabis.'

Note

A growing market: The domestic cultivation of cannabis by Mike Hough, Hamish Warburton, Bradley Few, Tiggey May, Lan-Ho Man, John Witton and Paul J. Turnbull is published by the Joseph Rowntree Foundation and available from York Publishing Services, 64 Hallfield Road, York YO31 7ZQ Tel: 01904 430033, price £13.95 plus £2 p&p.

■ The above information is from the Joseph Rowntree Foundation's web site which can be found at www.jrf.org.uk

Mixed signals

One man cleared of supplying drug. By Lucy Glynn

A man who admitted giving free cannabis to disabled people has been cleared of intending to supply the drug. Jeff Ditchfield, from Rhyl, North Wales, runs a shop selling cannabis paraphernalia.

Glyn Williams, from Caerwys, who has MS and has received cannabis from Mr Ditchfield, told Chester Crown Court in January that it reduces his pain more than any prescribed drug.

The jury found Mr Ditchfield not guilty, but the judge warned he could be prosecuted again if he continues to supply the drug.

Mr Ditchfield said afterwards: 'The jury understand I do it for sick people. It restored my faith in society. There are so many people relying on me for help. I get new people calling every day.'

A Legalise Cannabis Alliance spokesman said the case set 'a legal precedent', but a Crown Prosecution Service (CPS) spokeswoman said: 'This changes nothing for the CPS, but it may affect a judge's decision. If something is against the law, it remains against the law.'

The case came as cannabis was downgraded from a class B to class C drug, although it remains illegal.

Meanwhile, GW Pharmaceuticals has said it expects its cannabis spray to be licensed by the government's drug regulatory agency in June.

Cannabis reclassification – what it means

■ Both medicinal and recreational cannabis use are still illegal, but people found with a small amount are likely to be given a warning and have their cannabis confiscated. The government has not said what constitutes a 'small amount'.

■ Repeat offenders and people smoking cannabis near children are more likely to be arrested but whether they are or not depends on the individual police officer. Medicinal use might be taken into account.

■ The Association of Chief Police Officers expects a number of test cases will be brought against the police for unfair arrest. The outcome of these should help clarify the law.

■ Cannabis dealing still carries a maximum 14-year prison sentence.

■ The above information is from the magazine *Disability Now*'s web site which can be found at www.disabilitynow.org.uk

Life after reclassification

Information from the UK Cannabis Internet Activists (UKCIA)

As time has passed it has become apparent that what will happen in the real world after reclassification is more complicated than might have been expected from the simple movement of cannabis from class B to class C in the Misuse of Drugs Act. It is of course impossible to predict in a definite manner what will happen, but from the debates and legislation the Government has made and a set of guidelines the ACPO have released regarding how the cannabis laws should be enforced after reclassification we can see the likely outcome.

Cannabis possession, supply or growing will remain a criminal offence, punishable by various means including imprisonment.

The maximum prison sentence for simple possession of all types of cannabis and derivatives will be 2 years. All other forms of punishment currently in use, e.g. fines, cautions, community service etc., will still be able to be used against cannabis users. However, from the police officer's point of view, there will be a 'presumption against arrest' if a person is found to possess a small amount of cannabis and no other offence has been committed. However, you won't just be able go on your way – your cannabis will be confiscated by the officer and your identification details (e.g. name, address etc.) taken. If you refuse to provide any identification, or they don't believe what you say, you may be arrested. Identification is necessary because you may be arrested if you are found in possession of cannabis repeatedly.

The new legislation does allow for full arrest for cannabis possession to take place if the police officer so desires. Certain circumstances surrounding cannabis possession that are more likely to result in arrest have been given by the ACPO guidelines and are often referred to as 'aggravated possession'. These include:

- Where a person is smoking cannabis in public view.
- Where locally a person is known to be repeatedly dealt with for possession of cannabis.
- Persons who are in possession of cannabis under circumstances that are causing a locally identified policing problem.
- Persons in possession of cannabis inside or in the vicinity of premises frequented by young persons, e.g. schools, youth clubs, play areas.

In addition, if you are under 18 and found in possession of cannabis, you will be arrested. The Crime and Disorder Act requires youth offenders to be dealt with at a police station, so you will be arrested and taken to a police station. You may or may not just be reprimanded when you are there but you will initially be arrested.

There is no distinction between recreational and medical use, so the same rules will apply if you are using cannabis as a medicine. The Government has promised to license cannabis-based medication for use at some point in the future if it is approved by the necessary medical agencies but this is a separate issue from reclassification. Officially, despite evidence to the contrary, cannabis has no beneficial medical use and the laws reflect this. If and when such a licence is granted it is very unlikely it will permit general cannabis use for medical reasons – much more likely is the case where a specific medicine, e.g. GW Pharmaceuticals' 'Sativex', is permitted for specific illnesses.

The maximum prison sentence for cannabis supply remains at 14 years, as is currently the case, following an amendment to increase

---

There is no distinction between recreational and medical use, so the same rules will apply if you are using cannabis as a medicine

---

the punishment for supply of class C drugs to 14 years rather than the 5 it is at present. There is no new 'social supply' offence, so in the context of the legislation, passing a spliff around is the same legal offence of supply as importing and selling a ton of cannabis. Of course, as is the case now, your punishment is likely to reflect the severity of your 'crime'.

Little has been said about how growing cannabis will be dealt with. However, under the Misuse of Drugs Act 1971, a drug 'production' offence falls into the category of 'trafficking' and hence it seems likely that the maximum sentence for growing cannabis will remain at 14 years and there will be no assumption against arrest. A report called *The Domestic Cultivation of Cannabis* published by the Joseph Rowntree Foundation looked at alternatives for growing offences after reclassification, finding there were 'persuasive grounds for treating cultivation for personal use on a par with possession'. However, the Government has made no indication whatsoever that this will be the case.

There is no intention to permit coffee shops similar to those in Holland. It has been made clear that people trying to run such coffee shops will be arrested for supply if this offence takes place. Even if no supply or possession offence has been committed by the owner of such a shop, it is and will remain a separate offence to allow your premises to be used for smoking cannabis under section 8 of the Misuse of Drugs Act. Currently the punishment for allowing class C drugs to be used on your property is up to 5 years' imprisonment. It is unknown whether this will also be increased to 14 years upon reclassification, but it seems it certainly won't be reduced.

- The above information is an extract from the UKCIA's web site: www.ukcia.org

© UK Cannabis Internet Activists (UKCIA)

Use of cannabis for alleviation of MS symptoms

Information from the Multiple Sclerosis Society

The current position

Cannabis is an illegal drug. The Home Secretary has responsibility for this issue across the four nations of the UK.

People with MS have claimed that it has helped to relieve a number of the symptoms of MS including pain, stiffness and bladder problems.

A number of clinical trials have taken place. A commercial company – GW Pharmaceuticals – has carried out trials into nerve pain and general MS symptom relief. The Medical Research Council (MRC) carried out a major trial into muscle stiffness/spasms. A further trial into incontinence, funded by the MS Society, has yet to report.

Although the GW trials have finished they have yet to publish their data. GW is currently seeking a licence for its oral spray from the Medicines and Healthcare Products Regulatory Agency (MHRA).

The findings from the MRC Cannabis in MS trial (CAMS) found that cannabis-derived drug capsules had no significant effect on muscle spasticity, as measured by an independent assessment of spasticity. However, a majority of people with MS taking the drug felt that it had reduced the symptoms of their spasticity, as well as their pain. There was also some evidence that cannabis treatment led to improved mobility.

The National Institute for Clinical Excellence (NICE) has been asked to make recommendations for the NHS in England and Wales on the use of cannabis-based medicines for MS symptoms. However, the Institute will only appraise therapies that have been granted a licence from the regulatory agency (MHRA). Once GW can confirm they have been given regulatory approval for their product NICE will resume its appraisal.

Multiple Sclerosis Society

The position on recommending the use of cannabis-based medicines in Scotland and Northern Ireland is not clear.

What the MS Society thinks

Following the publications of the CAMS trial results, the Society said: 'The results of this large trial show the difficulty in assessing treatments for a variable and fluctuating condition like MS. Current methods of measurement do not always detect significant benefits patients may feel.

'Around two-thirds of those on the cannabis-derived medicines felt their spasticity was improved by them, even though that could not be shown clinically. More people on the drugs found relief from other very distressing symptoms like pain, spasm and sleeping problems than those taking a placebo.

'These improvements to quality of life can make a significant difference to people with MS, whose choice of treatments is very limited.

'On the evidence now available, the MS Society believes those who might benefit should be able to have treatment prescribed on the NHS. We also believe that further research into cannabis-derived medicines for MS should be vigorously pursued.'

The Home Secretary has already indicated he will take quick action to allow the prescription of licensed cannabis-based medicines which are proven to be both safe and effective.

When NICE resumes its appraisal, we shall be looking for the views of people with MS to be taken on board in arriving at a speedy verdict on the drugs.

In the meantime, the Society urges authorities to deal sympathetically with people who are self-medicating with cannabis to seek relief from the distressing symptoms of MS.

■ The above information is from the Multiple Sclerosis Society's web site: www.mssociety.org.uk

© Multiple Sclerosis Society
January 2004

NO, HONESTLY... IT *IS* JUST FOR MY *HEALTH*!

Medical cannabis

Information from the UK Cannabis Internet Activists

Perhaps the greatest injustice produced by the current legislation with regard to cannabis is that relating to its potential medical usage. The usage of cannabis is largely governed under the Misuse of Drugs Act 1971 and according to this it has no medical value. However, current scientific research and the testimonies of thousands of people from the past and present fully contradict this claim.

Cannabis has been used as a medicine worldwide for at least 5000 years. It was part of the British Formulary until 1971 when the Misuse of Drugs Act was passed, resulting in it being banned. The heyday of cannabis medicine was around the end of the nineteenth century, where it was used for a number of symptoms in a number of forms. The excitement of the introduction of hypodermic syringes and injectable opiates reduced its usage somewhat, in addition to newer synthetic drugs. However, in retrospect some of these new drugs have proved ineffective in some people, and have dangers inherent in their use. Unfortunately, the current state of our War on (some) Drugs legislative policies have prevented its legal use, and restricted any

Introduction

'Nearly all medicines have toxic, potentially lethal effects. But marijuana is not such a substance. There is no record in the extensive medical literature describing a proven, documented cannabis-induced fatality . . . Simply stated, researchers have been unable to give animals enough marijuana to induce death . . . In practical terms, marijuana cannot induce a lethal response as a result of drug-related toxicity . . . In strict medical terms marijuana is far safer than many foods we commonly consume . . . Marijuana, in its natural form, is one of the safest therapeutically active substances known to man.'

DEA Administrative Law Judge, FL Young, 1988

research efforts that brave scientists have attempted.

It seems almost farcical that currently in the UK, so-called hard drugs such as heroin and cocaine, whilst being illegal to use recreationally, are available on prescription whereas the relatively harmless cannabis plant cannot be used, it being deemed useless and too dangerous to use even under full medical supervision. This is no longer

a popular viewpoint. Several surveys have been done recently, and almost invariably they have come out with support for medical marijuana usage whether the survey is restricted to select groups (e.g. doctors) or to the general public. Indeed certain referendums in the United States have lead to some states (for example California and Arizona in 1996) 'legalising' cannabis for medicinal use. However, it is not a feasible solution as cannabis usage is still a federal crime.

Medicinal properties of cannabis

Cannabis has been claimed to help with a large number of wide-ranging symptoms. However, research has established three major properties which are medically useful. Cannabis is:

- an analgesic (relieves pain)
- an anti-emetic (relieves nausea and vomiting)
- an appetite stimulant (induces hunger).

As can be inferred from the bullets above, cannabis has a number of possible applications in medical treatment. Typically most research and use seem to focus on cancer chemotherapy, AIDS and MS. One

should not limit its possible applications to these symptoms however. Huge amounts of anecdotal evidence and increasing amounts of modern research suggest other uses as diverse as diseases of the body such as glaucoma, diseases of the mind such as Adult Attention Deficit Disorder and until-now untreatable conditions such as certain forms of tumour growth. Recent research also shows cannabis has anti-oxidative and neuro-protectional properties.

So why is cannabis not available on prescription?

This question may puzzle some readers! The simple answer is that cannabis cannot be prescribed for any reason due to the Misuse of Drugs Act.

Cannabis has been used as a medicine worldwide for at least 5000 years

---

This is evidently not a satisfactory answer. For a substance to become a 'medicine' and thus officially prescribable, it must be certified by the Medicines Control Agency as being suitable. This requires two measures – safety (harmfulness to the user) and efficacy (effectiveness for its designated purpose). However, cannabis has seemingly been repeatedly proved to be both safe and efficacious. In terms of safety, cannabis has never been proven to have caused even a single death directly. Its toxicity level is so low that no human has managed to consume enough to cause a fatal reaction.

This is extremely rare for modern medications. Every year, through overdoses, allergic reactions, contra-indications and for other reasons thousands of people die through the use of legitimately prescribed medications. According to National Institute on Drug Abuse (NIDA) statistics, the ubiquitous painkiller aspirin kills around 2000 people in America per year. As it has never been

accomplished it is unreliable, but experts have estimated that in order to ingest enough cannabis to die from its toxicity, you would need to have literally several thousands of times the quantity that people would use to medicate or during recreation. Compare these with legal drugs – aspirin for instance could be fatal (and is certainly very damaging) if just 20 times the recommended dose is taken. As for its effectiveness, ignoring the legal status, time and time again it is proven to help. Thousands of people testify to how it has helped them, and research is continually done which shows significant medical benefits in a wide array of disorders.

As time moves on, the serious issue of using cannabis medically becomes taken more and more seriously. Not only do people go out of their way to treat themselves with cannabis despite the possible consequences of law-breaking, but now a company has been set up specifically to research the possible therapeutic usages of cannabis. GW Pharmaceuticals is now (legally) conducting research into medical uses of cannabis. They have encountered no significant unexpected health-related problems, and are conducting trials with the hope of getting a cannabis-based medicine licensed for prescription usage within 3 years. They will apply for the licence in the near future, and the UK Government has indicated that if granted, they will allow the medicine to become legal to prescribe.

In July 2001, Canada became the first country to legalise cannabis for medical use. In Canada, cannabis can be legally prescribed by doctors, albeit under heavy restrictions. People with terminal illnesses, having less than a year to live, as well as those with certain specified conditions (for example AIDS, arthritis, cancer) will be allowed to use cannabis medicinally if they have a form signed by their doctor and two other experts. Unfortunately at this time it may be hard for some people to use it medicinally in practice due to lack of supply. The licensed patient or a named representative can grow cannabis for their usage, but no one else is allowed to cultivate or sell any form of cannabis for any reason. However, the Government has funded a cannabis plantation which mainly produces materials for research purposes and in the future it is likely that medical patients will be able to get their cannabis from them.

As time moves on, the serious issue of using cannabis medically becomes taken more and more seriously

---

Whatever the case, it should be remembered that whatever anyone's personal views are on the subject, thousands of people do treat themselves medically with cannabis. They spend excessive amounts of time and money in order to get their supply, without any guarantee of its strength, quality or purity. They risk confiscation, fines, criminal records and imprisonment. Why would they do this if cannabis was not an effective medication – indeed so effective it is worth risking everything rather than use a medication that the authorities have deemed 'legal'?

■ The above information is from the UK Cannabis Internet Activists' web site which can be found at www.ukcia.org

© UK Cannabis Internet Activists

Cannabis-based medicines

Cannabinoids and cannabis-based medicines. Information from GW Pharmaceuticals

Which particular cannabis plants has GW been working with?

The absolute requirement for a plant-based medicine from a regulatory point of view is 'control of starting materials'. A drug in its manufacture goes through many processes, each of which needs to be monitored and strict quality controls applied. This process control and QC would be invalidated if the starting materials (i.e. the herbal materials) were of poor or inconsistent quality.

GW's foremost consideration therefore is the cultivation of highly consistent plants with defined cannabinoid ratios. Total yield of one or other cannabinoid is relatively less important than consistency. We have a number of chemovars (varieties characterised by their chemical content) chosen for their composition and morphological traits i.e. hybrid vigour and disease resistance.

We are currently producing significant quantities of THC, CBD (cannabidiol), THC-V (the propyl anologue of THC), CBC-V (the propyl analogue of cannabichromene) and CBG (cannabigerol). Nothing is known of the pharmacology and possible therapeutic effects of CBC and CBG specifically.

Our clinical programme is comparing a number of cannabinoid ratios against placebo in each illness to establish which ratios are most suitable for each patient group.

What is a 'whole plant extract'?

When we talk about a 'whole plant extract' we mean an extract of the chosen part of the plant, and here we are talking about the aerial part of the plant, not the roots. We do not actually have to strip one part of the plant away; we are quite content to make extracts from all of the aerial parts of the plant – the leaf and the bud. Since our bud to leaf ratio is ten to one, we do not have much leaf.

By extraction we arrive at a pharmaceutical grade material which is a clear liquid in a bottle and from there we can proceed to formulation work and continue to incorporate those materials in the appropriate drug delivery modalities.

What are cannabinoids?

Cannabinoids are a group of molecules found only in the cannabis plant. Different cannabinoids appear to have different pharmacological effects but certain cannabinoids have been shown to have analgesic, anti-spasmodic, anti-convulsant, anti-tremor, anti-psychotic, anti-inflammatory, anti-oxidant, anti-emetic and appetite-stimulant properties and research is ongoing into neuro-protective and immunomodulatory effects.

What are GW's medicines?

GW's medicines are derived from standardised whole extracts of proprietary cannabis plant varieties bred to exhibit a pre-determined content of cannabinoids. These extracts are incorporated into non-smoked drug delivery technologies and then undergo pre-clinical and clinical testing prior to submitting applications to pharmaceutical regulatory authorities.

How is cannabis likely to be administered to patients?

GW's first product, Sativex®, is an oro-mucosal spray. GW is also evaluating tablet and capsule formulations and is developing an inhaler.

GW's medicines are derived from standardised whole extracts of proprietary cannabis plant varieties bred to exhibit a pre-determined content of cannabinoids

---

Why not just let patients smoke cannabis?

In GW's opinion, smoking is not an acceptable means of delivery for a medicine. Patients wish to use a medicine that is legally prescribed, does not require smoking, is of guaranteed quality, has been developed and approved by regulatory authorities for use in their specific medical condition and is dispensed by pharmacists under the supervision of their doctor.

Are cannabis medicines safe?

Data from GW's clinical trials confirm that its medicines are generally well tolerated. The trials have generated over 600 patient-years of safety data and adverse events have been predictable and generally well tolerated.

If GW's medicines become legal, will cannabis be legal?

No. A regulatory approval from the UK Medicines and Healthcare Products Regulatory Agency (MHRA) would be followed by a change in UK law allowing doctors to prescribe the MHRA-approved medication. This change in law would apply only to such an approved product and would have no direct consequence for the legal status of herbal cannabis for recreational and medical use.

How will these cannabis medicines become legal?

The UK Government has stated repeatedly that it will permit, subject to regulatory approval from the MHRA, cannabis-based medicines to be re-scheduled under the Misuse of Drugs Regulations so as to enable their general prescription. These changes can be made swiftly. Similar procedures apply in other countries around the world.

Do patients get high?

By careful self-titration (dose adjustment), most patients are able to separate the thresholds for symptom relief and intoxication, the 'therapeutic window', so enabling them to obtain symptom relief without experiencing a 'high'. Patients emphasise that they seek to obtain the medical benefits without intoxication.

Is GW looking at different forms of cannabis from those known to recreational users of the drug?

Recreationally, everybody has been trying to produce high THC varieties. We believe very strongly that many of the advantages of using the whole plant come from the inclusion of other components of cannabis in addition to THC, specifically CBD.

In the cannabis plant, it appears that some of the components added together give better effect. Some components seem to work to counteract some of the side effects of others, and the whole plant is generally well tolerated by humans. The relationship between the dose required for medicine and the dose required to kill somebody is about 20-40,000 times. A standard pharmaceutical ratio might be in the order of 50 or 100, so cannabis is in relative terms very well tolerated.

GW is interested in researching as many of the cannabinoids as possible. We are also interested in some of the non-cannabinoid contents. There are some ingredients in cannabis that have very potent pharmacological activity but which are not cannabinoids.

What is the current status of the GW research programme?

GW's clinical trials programme, which is independent of Government funding, is being carried out by a team of pharmaceutical professionals experienced in drug development and, in particular, the development of plant-based medicines and drug delivery systems. GW's team is also supported by a number of prominent scientific advisers in this field in Europe and North America.

In general, each step that is taken to produce a pharmaceutical needs to be tested under a range of conditions including extremes to simulate error. The test methods themselves need to be validated across the range of values expected. A development programme for regulatory approval has three main objectives: quality, safety and efficacy.

Quality relates to consistency of the product throughout production and in its final presentation and packaging. This will also include long-term testing of stability in order to establish an acceptable shelf life. The starting material will need to be tested for contaminants (which should be absent) such as pesticide and fungicide residues, fungal and microbial toxins, heavy metals, etc. Each test is performed many times.

Safety cannot rely solely on many years of vernacular use. Regulatory authorities require evidence from controlled studies and in-depth critical review of the literature by experts in order to assess safety. GW has embarked upon this costly and time-consuming undertaking to be able to provide sufficient evidence of appropriate quality to satisfy the regulatory authorities. The safety of the drug in clinical usage is continually monitored throughout the entire clinical development programme.

Efficacy: Prior to submission of our dossier for regulatory approval there are three phases of clinical research:

Phase I.

These are studies generally in healthy volunteers where the safe dose range of the drug is established. Phase I programmes are typically run in dedicated clinical pharmacology departments which do nothing but early-phase safety studies. Subjects may be exposed to increasing doses of the drug whilst all bodily functions are closely observed and blood samples taken to assess blood levels of the drug. Sometimes subjects are asked to perform tasks (e.g. exercise) or, more appropriately for cannabis-

based medicines, batteries of intensive cognitive and psychometric function testing. The data from these studies assist in establishing appropriate dosage schedules to be used in the Phase II studies.

Phase II.

These studies are generally carried out in small groups of patients. Usually specific aspects of the patient's condition are studied to demonstrate the effect, if any, of the drug on defined endpoints and to establish a dose/response relationship if present. In these studies the clinical endpoints are validated for their use in larger studies (i.e. are we asking the right questions or doing the right test to best evaluate the therapeutic value of the drug under test?). Some drugs which are seemingly similar may require very different measures of efficacy. We suspect cannabis may well be one that requires very close attention to the clinical endpoints.

Phase III.

Having established an acceptable dose range and validated the clinical endpoint in a range of conditions and having shown therapeutic benefit in the smaller Phase II studies then larger-scale studies are undertaken. Hundreds of patients may be entered into each study and may receive active or placebo or active and placebo in a random order. Subgroups of responding patients are identified and so are interactions with other medicines that the patient may take. Special target patient groups will be studied at this time – young, old, renal impaired etc.

GW has now completed a number of Phase III clinical trials and has further Phase III trials under way.

When will a cannabis medicine be ready for market?

In March 2003 GW submitted an application to the UK Medicines and Healthcare Products Regulatory Agency (MHRA) for our lead product, Sativex®. This application is currently going through the normal review process.

■ The above information is from GW Pharmaceuticals' web site which can be found at www.gwpharm.com
© *GW Pharmaceuticals 2004*

■ Cannabis is one of the world's most commonly used leisure drugs. It's estimated that at least one person in 20 in the UK has used it. (p. 1)

■ Cannabis comes in three main forms: cannabis resin, marijuana/grass and cannabis oil. (p. 1)

■ The mind-altering ingredient is a substance called delta 9 tetra-hydrocannabinol (THC). The main types of cannabis vary greatly in their strength, depending on the concentration of THC. (p. 1)

■ The most commonly used drug by young people was cannabis, which had been used by 33 per cent of young men and 21 per cent of young women in the previous year. (p. 2)

■ The debate about the law on cannabis centres on a number of important legal and social issues concerning civil liberties and personal choice, legal coherence and international agreements. (p. 5)

■ Arguments about cannabis seem to fall into two camps: some people are determined that it is harmless and others say it is very dangerous. The truth seems to fall somewhere between these two extremes. (p. 7)

■ The impact on mental wellbeing is one of the biggest concerns about cannabis. Some experts are concerned that cannabis use can cause a range of mental health problems. (p. 7)

■ Cannabis is still illegal! In January 2004, cannabis was moved from class B to class C. However, it remains illegal to possess, grow, supply cannabis or to allow it to be smoked on your premises. (p. 7)

■ Research has revealed that Britain's 'cannabis economy' is worth £5 billion a year in sales alone. (p. 8)

■ It has been argued that cannabis smoke contains carcinogenic substances. The British Lung Foundation recently reported that smoking 3 cannabis 'joints' was equivalent to 20 cigarettes. (p. 10)

■ Although the evidence is not conclusive, some research has suggested that cannabis can stimulate mental health disorders such as schizophrenia. (p. 10)

■ Cannabis remains the illicit drug most frequently used by young people across Europe. The UK has one of the highest usage levels in Europe, with 42% of all 15- to 34-year-olds saying they had tried it at least once – second only to Denmark. (p. 11)

■ It has been estimated that approximately 10% of those who use cannabis become dependent. On the other hand, the majority of cannabis users quit before the age of 30. (p. 13)

■ Cannabis may exacerbate the illnesses of those suffering from emphysema, bronchitis, schizophrenia and alcohol and other drug dependencies. (p. 15)

■ A Dutch study of 4,000 people from the general population found that those taking large amounts of cannabis were almost seven times more likely to have psychotic symptoms three years later. (p. 17)

■ Nearly 80 per cent of those who had driven while or after using cannabis said they would be deterred from doing so if roadside testing were introduced. (p. 21)

■ The Netherlands yesterday became the first country to legalise the medical use of cannabis, allowing doctors to prescribe the narcotic as a painkiller for those who are seriously ill. (p. 22)

■ Simple possession now carries a maximum two-year custodial sentence or a fine. (p. 23)

■ The penalty for supply offences has increased from 5 years' to 14 years' imprisonment. (p. 23)

■ The law has not changed in relation to young people and cannabis. Young people caught in possession of cannabis WILL STILL be arrested under the Crime and Disorder Act [1998] which requires young offenders to be dealt with at the police station. (p. 23)

■ Being unfit to drive under the influence of any intoxicant, including cannabis, is an offence which is likely to lead to the loss of your driving licence. Getting your licence back and obtaining insurance after losing it are likely to be difficult. (p. 23)

■ Those who smoke openly in public face possible arrest and prosecution. (p. 25)

■ Home cultivation of cannabis is so widespread that it may now account for as much as half of all consumption in Britain. (p. 32)

■ Home Office statistics show that 458 offenders were cautioned for cannabis cultivation in 2000, while another 1,502 were convicted in court, including 243 who were sent to prison. (p. 32)

■ People with MS have claimed that it has helped to relieve a number of the symptoms of MS including pain, stiffness and bladder problems. (p. 35)

■ Cannabis has been used as a medicine worldwide for at least 5000 years. (p. 36)

ADDITIONAL RESOURCES

You might like to contact the following organisations for further information. Due to the increasing cost of postage, many organisations cannot respond to enquiries unless they receive a stamped, addressed envelope.

Association of Chief Police Officers (ACPO)
25 Victoria Street
London, SW1H 0EX
Tel: 020 7227 3434
Fax: 020 7227 3400
E-mail: info@acpo.police.uk
Web site: www.acpo.police.uk
ACPO was set up so that work in developing policing policies could be undertaken in one place, on behalf of the service as a whole.

Beckley Foundation
Beckley Park
Oxford, OX3 9SY
Tel: 01865 351209
E-mail: office@beckleyfoundation.org
Web site: www.beckleyfoundation.co.uk
The Beckley Foundation supports a programme of experimental research at leading scientific research institutions both in the UK and abroad.

The Christian Institute
26 Jesmond Road
Newcastle upon Tyne, NE2 4PQ
Tel: 0191 281 5664
Fax: 0191 281 4272
E-mail: info@christian.org.uk
Web site: www.christian.org.uk
The Christian Institute is a registered charity that seeks to promote the Christian faith in the United Kingdom.

Disability Now
6 Market Road
London, N7 9PW
Tel: 020 7619 7323
Fax: 020 7619 7331
Web site: www.disabilitynow.org.uk
The UK's leading disability newspaper.

DrugScope
Waterbridge House
32-36 Loman Street
London, SE1 0EE
Tel: 020 7928 1211
Fax: 020 7928 1771
E-mail: services@drugscope.org.uk
Web site: www.drugscope.org.uk

DrugScope is the UK's leading independent centre of expertise on drugs.

Economic and Social Research Council (ESRC)
Polaris House
North Star Avenue
Swindon
Wiltshire, SN2 1UJ
Tel: 01793 413000
Fax: 01793 413130
E-mail: exrel@esrc.ac.uk
Web site: www.esrc.ac.uk
The ESRC is the UK's largest independent funding agency for research and postgraduate training into social and economic issues.

European Monitoring Centre for Drugs and Drug Addiction (EMCDDA)
Rua da Cruz de Santa Apolónia 23-25 , PT-1149-045 Lisboa, Portugal
Tel: + 351 21 811 3032
Fax: + 351 21 813 1711
E-mail: info@emcdda.eu.int
Web site: www.emcdda.eu.int
EMCDDA provides objective, reliable and comparable information at European level concerning drugs and drug addiction and their consequences.

GW Pharmaceuticals plc
Porton Down Science Park
Salisbury
Wiltshire, SP4 0JQ
Tel: 01980 557000
Fax: 01980 557111
E-mail: info@gwpharm.com
Web site: www.gwpharm.com
GW Pharmaceuticals is licensed by the UK Home Office to work with a range of controlled drugs for medical research purposes.

Joseph Rowntree Foundation (JRF)
The Homestead
40 Water End
York, YO30 6WP
Tel: 01904 629241
Fax: 01904 620072
E-mail: infor@jrf.org.uk

Web site: www.jrf.org.uk
JRF is an independent, non-political body which funds programmes of research and innovative development in the fields of housing, social care and social policy.

The Maranatha Community
102 Irlam Road, Flixton
Manchester, M41 6JT
Tel: 0161 748 4858
Fax: 0161 747 7379
E-mail: office@maranatha community.freeserve.co.uk
Web site: www.maranathacommunity.org.uk
A Christian movement which involves members of many different strands within the Christian faith.

Multiple Sclerosis Society
MS National Centre
372 Edgware Road
London, NW2 6ND
Tel: 020 8438 0700
Web site: www.mssociety.org.uk
The MS Society is the UK's largest charity for people affected by Multiple Sclerosis (MS).

Release
388 Old Street
London, EC1V 9LT
Tel: 020 7729 9904
Fax: 020 7729 2599
E-mail: info@release.org.uk
Web site: www.release.org.uk
Release provides a range of services dedicated to meeting the health, welfare and legal needs of drugs users and those who live and work with them.

Rethink
National Office
28 Castle Street
Kingston-upon-Thames
Surrey, KT1 1SS
Tel: 020 8547 3937
Fax: 020 8547 3862
E-mail: info@rethink.org
Web site: www.rethink.org
Rethink is the largest severe mental illness charity in the UK.

age, and attitudes to illegal drugs 27-8
alcohol
    and cannabis users 8-9, 21
    deaths caused by 10
    and other drugs 26
aspirin, toxicity levels compared to cannabis 37

bipolar affective disorder (manic depression), and
    cannabis 14
Blunkett, David, and cannabis reclassification 20, 28, 29,
    31, 32
boys and young men, and cannabis use 2, 3, 11
British Crime Survey (BCS), on cannabis use 2, 4, 6, 18, 28
British Medical Association (BMA), on the health effects
    of cannabis 29

Canada, legalisation of the medicinal use of cannabis 37
cancer
    and cannabis use 10, 12, 13, 26
        medicinal 37
cannabis
    arguments against 12
    cafés 25, 34
    and the cannabis economy 8-9, 18
    cannabis oil 1, 4, 6
    cannabis resin 1, 4, 6, 7
        price of 11
        'soap' 6, 7
    constituents of 18
    deaths 16-17, 20
    dependence on 2, 12, 19, 21, 26
    eating 1, 4, 18, 20
    effects of 1-2
        on the brain 13, 18
        on learning and educational performance 19
    facts and urban myths 6-7
    and the gateway theory 9, 26, 28
    and hard drug use 9-10, 29-30
    and health 7, 10, 12, 13, 15
        information for GPs 18-20
        and reclassification 29, 30
    herbal cannabis (marijuana/grass) 1, 4, 6, 11
    home cultivation of 32-3, 34
    legal position on 23
    legalisation debate 4-6
        civil liberties and personal choice 5
        implications of changing the law in one nation 5
        and the police and judiciary 5
        and political parties 4
        and practical details 6
        and public opinion 4-5, 27-8
    medicinal use of 5, 7, 12, 22, 34, 35-9
        Government policy on 26, 34
        GW Pharmaceuticals trials 26, 35, 37, 38-9
        and home cultivation 32
        and multiple sclerosis 35

    as a painkiller 22, 26, 37
    and mental health 7, 10, 12, 13, 14, 16, 19-20, 26
        links to psychosis 17, 19
    misconceptions 9-10
    names for 4
    potency of 6, 11, 12, 20
    prices 6, 11
    reclassification of 7, 8, 14, 18, 20
        arguments for and against 28
        and disabled people 33
        government advertising on 29-30
        life after 34
        public opinion on 27-8
        questions and answers on 24-6
    risks of 2
    seizures of 2, 3
    side effects of 2
    smoking 1, 2, 4
        cannabis cigarettes 9
        health risks of 7, 12, 13, 18-19
    stages of intoxication 13
    testing for 2
    THC content of 2, 3, 4, 6-7, 11, 13, 15, 18, 19
        and cannabis medicines 39
    toxicity levels compared to aspirin 37
    and the treatment demand indicator (TDI) 3
    users
        age of quitting 13
        and driving 2, 12, 13, 16, 17, 19, 21
        in EU countries 3, 11
        lifetime prevalence 3
        on negative effects of 22
        on positive effects of 21-2
        statistics on 2, 3, 4, 6, 9, 18
        young people in the UK 11
    what it looks like 1, 4
    where it comes from 6
cigarettes
    and cannabis users 26
    deaths caused by 10
    development of cannabis 9
civil liberties, and the cannabis legalisation debate 5
cocaine, use by young people 2
consumers, and cannabis economy 8-9
crime, and drug abuse 28

deaths
    and drug misuse 10, 11
        cannabis 16-17, 20
depression, and cannabis 7, 16, 22
disabled people, supplying cannabis to 33
doctors *see* GPs (general practitioners)
driving
    and cannabis
        effects of 2, 12, 13, 16, 17, 19, 21
        law on 23

drug abuse
    and the classification of drugs 24
    public attitudes to 27-8
    statistics on 2
    see also cannabis
drug seizures, statistics 2
drug testing, for cannabis 2

eastern Europe, cannabis use in 11
ecstasy, deaths from 10, 11
European Union (EU)
    cannabis use in EU countries 3, 11
    and legalisation 5, 11

fast food, and the cannabis economy 8

Government policies
    on cannabis
        advertising 29-30
        Home Office awareness campaign 14, 24
        for medicinal purposes 26, 34
        national campaign (FRANK) 26
        reclassification of 7, 8, 14, 18, 20, 24-6
GPs (general practitioners)
    and the adverse affects of cannabis, advice to patients
    18-19
    prescribing cannabis to patients
        and the law 7
        support for 5

health
    and cannabis 7, 10, 12, 13, 15
        acute and chronic effects 15
        and the immune system 19
        information for GPs 18-20
        lung damage 18-19
        and pregnant women 15, 19
        reclassification of 29, 30
    see also mental health
herbal cannabis (marijuana/grass) 1, 4
    cost of 6
    potency of 6, 11
    where it comes from 6

medicinal use of cannabis 5, 7, 12, 22, 34, 35-9
    as an anti-emetic 37
    as an appetite stimulant 37
    in Canada 37
    and cannabinoids 38
    and cannabis reclassification 34
    Government policy on 26, 34
    GW Pharmaceuticals trials 26, 35, 37, 38-9
      phases of 39
    history of 36
    and home cultivation 32
    and intoxication 39
    legality of 38-9
    and multiple sclerosis (MS) 35
    as a painkiller 22, 26, 37
    public attitudes to 36
    safety of 38

and smoking 38
and terminal illnesses 37
types of cannabis plants used in 38
and 'whole plant extract' 38
mental health
    and cannabis 7, 10, 12, 13, 14, 16, 19-20, 26
        deaths 16
        links to psychosis 17, 19
multiple sclerosis (MS), and the medicinal use of
    cannabis 35

National Institute for Clinical Excellence (NICE), and
    cannabis-based medicines 35

pain relief, cannabis as a painkiller 22, 26, 37
police
    and cannabis
        guidelines on policing 30, 31, 34
        home cultivation of 32-3
        possession 5, 7, 8, 23, 24-5, 30
        powers of arrest 30, 31, 34
        reclassification 29-30, 34
        and under 18s 7, 25, 30, 31, 34
    and driving by cannabis users 21
political parties, and the cannabis legalisation debate 4
pregnant women, and cannabis 15, 19
prison sentences, for cannabis possession 30, 34
psychosis, cannabis link to 17, 19

road traffic accidents, and cannabis 16, 17

schizophrenia, and cannabis 7, 10, 12, 14, 17, 19-20, 22, 26
school exclusions, and cannabis 7
sentences, for cannabis possession/supply 23, 24, 30
solvent abuse 11
suicide, and cannabis 16

television, and cannabis users 9
terminal illnesses, and the medicinal use of cannabis 37
tetrahydrocannabinol (THC) in cannabis 2, 3, 4, 6-7,
    11, 13, 15, 18, 19
    and cannabis medicine 39

United Nations, convention on Narcotic Drugs 5
United States, and the medicinal use of cannabis 36

women
    pregnant women and cannabis 15, 19
    young women and cannabis 2
workplace, and cannabis users 22

young people
    and cannabis 3, 18
        attitudes to addictive drugs 27
        and the cannabis economy 8-9
        deaths 16
        Government policies on 25, 26
        home cultivation of 33
        Home Office awareness campaign 14
        and the legalisation debate 5
        and market saturation 11
        and mental illness 17
        under 18s and the police 7, 25, 30, 31, 34
Youth Offending Teams (YOTs), and cannabis users 7, 25

ACKNOWLEDGEMENTS

The publisher is grateful for permission to reproduce the following material.

While every care has been taken to trace and acknowledge copyright, the publisher tenders its apology for any accidental infringement or where copyright has proved untraceable. The publisher would be pleased to come to a suitable arrangement in any such case with the rightful owner.

Chapter One: The Facts of Cannabis

Cannabis/Dope/Marijuana/Skunk/Grass, © Release, *One in three young men use cannabis*, © Crown copyright is reproduced with the permission of Her Majesty's Stationery Office, *Drug misuse*, © Crown copyright is reproduced with the permission of Her Majesty's Stationery Office, *Cannabis trends*, © European Monitoring Centre for Drugs and Drug Addiction (EMCDDA), *Drug use among young adults*, © European Monitoring Centre for Drugs and Drug Addiction (EMCDDA), *Cannabis*, © DrugScope, *Cannabis – facts and urban myths*, © Kevin Flemen, KFx Drugs Awareness, *So how many people use cannabis in the UK?*, © Crown copyright is reproduced with the permission of Her Majesty's Stationery Office, *Cannabis economy brings in £11bn*, © Guardian Newspapers Limited 2003, *Cannabis misconceptions*, © DrugScope, *Drugs and harm*, © YouGov Poll, *The cannabis market*, © Guardian Newspapers Limited 2003, *Cannabis – the lies and the truth*, © Maranatha Community, *Cannabis – a soft drug?*, © Beckley Foundation, *Cannabis and mental health*, © Rethink, *Cannabis-related harms on health*, © DrugScope, *Addiction*, © YouGov Poll, *Cannabis deaths*, © Telegraph Group Limited, London 2004, *Drug-related poisoning deaths*, © Crown copyright is reproduced with the permission of Her Majesty's Stationery Office, *Cannabis link to psychosis*, © Guardian Newspapers Limited 2003, *Cannabis for the GP*, © Maranatha Community, *Cannabis is blamed as cause of man's death*, © Telegraph Group Limited, London 2004, *Drug-driving*, © Dr Philip Terry, *Medical use of cannabis approved*, © Guardian Newspapers Limited 2003.

Chapter Two: The Legal Debate

The legal position on cannabis, © Release, *Cannabis reclassification*, © Crown copyright is reproduced with the permission of Her Majesty's Stationery Office, *Cannabis and the law*, © Telegraph Group Limited, London 2004, *Drugs and the law*, © YouGov Poll, *Simple and powerful rebuttals of common arguments*, © The Christian Institute, October 2003, *Government ads aim to end confusion*, © Guardian Newspapers Limited 2003, *ACPO publish cannabis enforcement guidelines*, © ACPO, *Policing cannabis*, © Telegraph Group Limited, London 2004, *Seizures of selected drugs*, © Crown copyright is reproduced with the permission of Her Majesty's Stationery Office, *Home cultivation of cannabis*, © Joseph Rowntree Foundation, *Mixed signals*, © Disability Now, *Life after reclassification*, © UK Cannabis Internet Activists (UKCIA), *Use of cannabis for alleviation of MS symptoms*, © Multiple Sclerosis Society, *Medical cannabis*, © UK Cannabis Internet Activists (UKCIA), *Cannabis-based medicines*, © GW Pharmaceuticals 2004.

Photographs and illustrations:

Pages 1, 21, 26, 29, 36: Simon Kneebone; pages 4, 19, 32: Pumpkin House; page 8: Angelo Madrid; pages 14, 25, 35: Bev Aisbett; page 23: Don Hatcher.

Craig Donnellan
Cambridge
April, 2004